Droitwich Golf Club

1897-1997

The first clubhouse in Bays Meadow, 1898

Droitwich Golf Club

1897-1997

by

John Bromhead

Grant Books, Worcestershire 1996

ISBN 0 907 186 90 4

Hughes & Company, Printers
Kempsey, Worcestershire

Published in a limited edition of 700 copies
by
Grant Books
The Coach House, Cutnall Green,
Droitwich, Worcestershire WR9 0PQ

Droitwich Golf Club

1897-1997

Published in a limited edition of
700 copies

Copy No:

Grant Books
Worcestershire 1996

Contents

Acknowledgements

The author has gained much insight and information from discussions with many members for which he is very grateful and without which the text would have been the poorer. Other contributions are acknowledged in the list of references.

Oral reminiscences

Mr. Ray Baldwin, Mr. John Baylis, Mr. Ivan Bedford, Mr. John Bickerton,
Mr. John Bickerton Jun., Mr. Geoff Bill, Mrs. Kitty Bill, Mr. Jim Bourne,
Mr. John Brackston, Mr. Colin Brade, Mr. Enos Colley, Miss Nellie Copson,
Mr. Tony Cox, Mr. Brian Croydon, Mr. Warren Davies, Mr. Mike Deeley,
Mr. Cyril Duggan, Mrs. Pat Duggan, Mr. Norman Edwards,
Mr. Cecil Everton, Mr. Derek Fellows, Mrs. Brenda Fowler, Mr. John Freeman,
Mr. Bob Gould, Mr. Jim Gray, Mrs. Sylvia Gray, Mr. Arthur Guise,
Mr. Pete Handy, Mr. Bryn Harrington, Mr. Percy Harris, Mr. David Hill,
Air Commodore Peter Hughes C.B.E., D.F.C., Group Captain A.F. Jackson,
Mr. Barry Joule, Miss Marian Lewis, Mr. 'Pop' Lewis, Mr. Albert Lippett,
Mrs. Billie Lippett, Mr. Hamish Macdonald, Mr. Gordon McDougall,
Mr. Alan Nicholls, Mr. Tony Phillips, Mr. Derek Platts, Mr. Bernard Preston,
Mr. David Rea, Mr. Ian Rone, Mr. Bill Ross, Mr. Jack Russell, Mr. Mike Shaw,
Mr. Terry Shingler, Mrs. G.M. Stretton-Cox, The Rev. Marian Talbot,
Mr. Mike Taylor, Mr. Andrew Terry, Mr. Chris Thompson, Mr. Bob Tunstall,
Mr. Ron Wall, Mr. Dave Walsh, Mrs. Ros Weston, Mr. Roy Whitehouse,
Mrs. Betty Whiting, Mr. Ray Woodhead.

Many of those named above have also lent photographs and other items.
In addition we must thank;
Mrs. Betty Bourne, Charles and Brian Buckle, Simon Braithwaite, John Eddiford,
Mrs. Helen Godber, G.N. Hopcraft, Len Johnson, Mr. C. Mills,
John Mole, Dr G. Shirley Jones and David Tilt.

The sketches are by Wayne Dutton.

Secretarial and other professional assistance

Mrs. Margaret Bromhead, Miss Nellie Copson, Mr. John Fitzgerald,
Mrs. Marion Lancaster, Mr. Peter N. Lewis (British Golf Museum, St. Andrews),
Mr. Jamie A.H. Peart (Map Librarian, University of Birmingham),
Mrs. Brenda Smith (Worcestershire Union of Golf Clubs), Mrs. Mary Wightman.

Message from the Chairman

I<small>T WAS</small> originally believed that Droitwich Golf Club was formed in 1895 and on this assumption a centenary committee was set up in 1993 to start preparing for our celebrations. Soon after John Bromhead began his research for this book he discovered that the actual decision to form Droitwich Golf Club was made on the 21st November 1896 and that golf did not start until 1897. This book tells the story of those beginnings and of the events and growth of the past 100 years.

We have today an excellent golf course and, with the completion of our new west wing, facilities equal to those of any other club in the county. This has been brought about by the foresight and dedication of our predecessors who gave freely of their time and effort to make it what it is today and it is up to all of us to ensure that it continues.

We would wish to express our gratitude to the family of the late A. V. Brackston for making available the invaluable memoirs and notes of 'Brackie' without which much of our history would be incomplete.

We are also deeply indebted to John Bromhead for the enormous amount of time and persistence he has put in over the last three years in gathering the material for this book and for preparing it with care and accuracy to present a comprehensive story. He has received support and assistance from his fellow members of the book committee under the chairmanship of John Weston.

The result of these efforts is this book which gives a most informative and detailed account of the club's history.

I wish all our members and guests who visit us in 1997 a very happy centenary year.

G<small>EOFF</small> H<small>UDSPITH</small>
Chairman

Message from the Centenary Captain

I T IS indeed a great privilege and honour to be your captain in this our centenary year, chosen by a somewhat unique event in the recent history of the club, a democratic and very close ballot. From the following pages you will appreciate the tremendous achievements of those dedicated men and women whose investment and imagination formed the basis of the wonderful facility we have today. There were many lows and a few highs along the way professionally chronicled here in this absorbing book. It really is a fascinating read.

Golf has undoubtedly increased in popularity, particularly over the last quarter of a century. However, the modern trend has been channelled towards proprietary owned clubs where the emphasis is to profit and the financial interests of the shareholders. I hope, therefore, we can take pride and relish a warm feeling in belonging to a members' club such as ours that has the best interests of its members at heart. It is good to know that any contribution we care to make, however small or however time consuming, is to our ultimate benefit.

In the same way that we have experienced and still derive a great deal of pleasure from the efforts of our predecessors we should be mindful that we, in turn, have a duty to our successors. We must maintain the present success we have helped to create, continue the genial atmosphere we have in the clubhouse and support the upkeep of our beautiful course.

My final word in this brief message to you is to *Enjoy*. To complete a century of continuous golf at Droitwich is rather special. It is time for congratulations and celebrations - we are not going to experience this situation again - let us all set out to enjoy the occasion. I intend to enjoy, it is my sincere wish that you all do likewise.

WALTER JARVIS
Centenary Captain

Message from the Centenary Ladies' Captain

WHEN I think of all the club captains, ladies' captains and the members who have been associated with Droitwich over the last one hundred years it is indeed a great honour to be chosen as ladies' captain for our centenary year. I have been a member for twenty-seven years and can truthfully say I owe a great deal to the golf club in the way of my personal enjoyment. I have also made many dear friends. Our club is well known for its friendliness and that I can vouchsafe. As a Scot I am an incomer, but have never felt so.

I hope everyone has a marvellous time in 1997 but, while we are reaping the benefits of our centenary, let us be thankful to all those past members who have worked hard over the years to give us the course and the club we are all so proud of today. Long live Droitwich Golf and Country Club.

SYLVIA GRAY
Centenary Ladies' Captain

Preface

WRITING HISTORICALLY about Droitwich Golf Club is not new. There have been reports in the local newspapers from before day one, minutes of meetings have been recorded - although only recent minutes have survived, annual reports have been written (only a few of which, apart from recent years, still exist) and dear Brackie wrote eight pages entitled *A Short History of Droitwich Golf Club* (which ends when he retired from being Honorary Secretary in 1972).

In my research I have been very impressed by the enterprise which led to the founding of our club and the patronage of John Corbett and the Corbett Trustees but above all by the spirit of the members who have given much time and hard work, much skill and goodwill to the making and survival of the club.

Once the club had been established the highlights in the story have been the upgrading from a nine hole course to an eighteen hole course, the move from Bays Meadow to Westford House, the survival through two world wars and some very lean years and finally the conversion of the course into two loops of nine holes. The new west wing on the club house is a significant episode as we build up to the celebration of the centenary. The involvement of the ladies in the running of the club has been a marked feature of the club's administration going back to 1899 and we are not aware of another golf club having a lady on their committee as early as that.

The standing of the club in Worcestershire golf circles and the abilities of our members to play good golf have risen considerably in the last twenty-five years. The club has been very well served by a succession of devoted professionals and club secretaries.

The text covering the ladies, the seniors and the juniors has been written partly from my notes but mostly by the sections themselves. This book would not have been completed without the help of my wife, Margaret, who wrote the chapter on the business side of the club. Her hard work as research assistant and her moral support have been invaluable to me. I am most grateful also to Duncan Stuart and the chairman of our book committee, John Weston. John gave me a head start with the research and managed the illustrations; Duncan has an expertise with computers and contributed *The Seniors, The Centenary and Beyond* and the *Epilogue*. John Moreton has acted as editor and his work is much appreciated as is his chapter on the course.

I am pleased to acknowledge the input from many club members and club well-wishers in interviews and chats. Were I writing a library and not one volume I would have given lengthier tributes and included more people.

Selection of biographical facts has not always come naturally. It is all too easy to pass on too much detail on an individual thus 'distorting the significance of this personage relative to others mentioned in the account' (Arthur Marwick).[1] At least I did dip my toe into the muddied waters of interviewing members, an undertaking which some club historians have shunned altogether.

Droitwich Golf Club has been a popular place to visit, a happy place at which to work and a beautiful and enjoyable venue for playing golf at all levels. As I am an avid collector of quotations I shall pass on two further sayings, 'The present doesn't last, the future is uncertain and so all we are left with is history'[2] and finally from the pen of the late David Wightman: golf clubs 'exist to promote the challenge, fun and fellowship of the game'.[3]

If you have slaved many hours and contributed much of value to the club and have been influential but receive in these pages little or no mention, I am sorry. To compensate yourself focus on the span of one hundred years and know that you are in good company. Many before you have also served and also have no memorial except the very continuance and success of the club.

John Bromhead

CHAPTER ONE

Beginnings

'Go through the Vines to pleasant lines
Play your golf at pleasure
You'll always find a welcome kind
From Droitwich folk at leisure.' [4]

'WE MAY estimate that, since 1886, golfers have increased throughout Great Britain in the ratio of thirty to one' - so wrote A. Wallis Myers in 1906. [5] To cope with this increase, fourteen courses had opened in Worcestershire alone before the turn of the century. There are still only some thirty-three today.

On 21st November, 1896, the Mayor of Droitwich, Councillor Harry Shirley Jones, presided over a meeting at the Salters Hall. The local paper reported 'a very fair attendance' and 'it was resolved to start a golf club for Droitwich'. [6]

At this point it is necessary to clarify the date of the foundation of the club. *The Victoria County History of Worcestershire* cites 1895 as the year in which the club began, leading to the confusion about our centenary year. As we shall see, golf, as we know it, was first played at Droitwich in 1897.

Arrangements were made with the tenant, Mr T. W. Wall, for the conversion of land which he farmed in Bays Meadow. The owner of the land, Mr. John Corbett, also consented and he was duly elected president of the club. A committee was elected at the meeting, as were Mr. J. Harrison as honorary treasurer and Mr. J. E. Harrison as honorary secretary. The former was the manager of Lloyds Bank in the town. Councillor Harry Shirley Jones became chairman and was joined on the committee by fellow doctor Percy Austin Roden, Mr. Thomas Townsend and Mr. T.W. Wall. They resolved that a professional should be called in at once to lay out 'the links'.

George Cawsey, the professional at Kings Norton Golf Club, was chosen and he constructed a nine hole course on Bays Meadow, a short distance

The Droitwich Guardian

AND

BRINE BATHS RECORD

Saturday, November 28, 1896

A GOLF CLUB FOR DROITWICH

Golf links should be an acquisition to Droitwich Residents and visitors who are golf players have long pressed this upon us, and there is not the slightest doubt that they materially assist a town which lays itself out for the accommodation of visitors. Friends and relatives who come with rheumatic patients want something to help to pass away the time, and if they are golf players the links will call them. Others who come for rest and change from busy employments find golf just the sufficient exercise and recreation that they need. In choosing a place to spend a few weeks the fact that a town has golf links is a factor not to be despised, and "Ten minutes to the golf links" is an inducement that is not forgotten in advertisements. Hitherto lovers of the game have had to journey to Malvern, or may be to Bromsgrove, to enjoy the game which has taken such a hold upon its votaries. Now we are to have golf links of our own. By arrangement with Mr. CORBETT, and his tenant, Mr. T. WALL, Bays Meadow is to be converted into links. It has the great advantage of accessibility, and a professional player from King's Norton who has visited it this week reports most favourably upon its merits for links. It will accommodate nine holes, and the ground is sufficiently sporting to make some interesting games. Droitwich has its Cricket, Football, and Hockey Clubs Golf appeals not only to the young and active, but to those who cannot indulge in violent exercise, and ladies may indulge in it. It now remains to be seen whether this seductive game will exercise the charm in Droitwich that it has elsewhere.

A meeting was held in the Reading Room of the Salters' Hall (kindly lent for the occasion by Mr. J. Corbett), on Saturday night last to inaugurate a golf club. The Mayor (Councillor H. S. Jones) was in the chair, and there were also present : The Rev. H. J. Hammond, Dr. Cruickshank, Dr. Gocher, Dr. P. Roden, Mr. E. Townsend, Mr. J. J. Hossell, Mr. F. Holyoake, Mr. T. Young, Mr. J. E. Harrison, Mr. S. Culley, and Mr. T. W. Wall.

On the proposal of the MAYOR, it was resolved unanimously that a Golf Club be formed for Droitwich.

It transpired that a ground had been decided on, by kind permission of owner and tenant, in Bays Meadow.

The Mayor, Dr. Roden, and Messrs. Townsend, F. Holyoake, and T. W. Wall were elected a committee, with a view to the formation of links and the management generally of the Club.

Mr J. Harrison, of Lloyds Bank, was elected hon. treasurer ; and Mr J. E. Harrison hon. sec.

It was generally felt that the links would greatly add to the attractions of the town, and would prove a source of exercise to visitors staying in the borough.

A vote of thanks was accorded to the Mayor for presiding and the proceedings then terminated.

from the town. As there were only twenty one male and seven lady members, visitors to the Brine Baths were welcomed at the club, which was 'within ten minutes walk from the centre of town, sporting in character and well patronised'. [7]

The nine holes had a bogey score of 35 and were constructed upon pasture land with a stiff loam soil. Summer play, it was reported, was difficult and there were both natural and artificial hazards. Today's golfers should realise that the triplex mower is a modern invention; early golfers thought progress was being made when leather boots were provided to prevent the hooves of the horses pulling the gang-mowers from damaging the turf! At this time many courses were actually closed in summer months entirely because the grass had grown too long for the practicalities of playing the game.

The first 9 hole course in Bays Meadow showing the golf pavilion left of centre. This map survey carried out in 1901 also shows the railway station bottom left, where many visiting golfers arrived. Reproduced from the 1903 Ordnance Survey map.

3

The rise of golf during this decade was aided and abetted greatly by the growth of the railways and Peter Lewis, the curator of the British Golf Museum at St Andrews, has thrown light on this. [8] Droitwich was no exception to the national trend and the station was substantially upgraded. Droitwich Golf Club was declared open for play in the *Bromsgrove, Droitwich and Redditch Weekly Messenger* of Saturday, 30th January, 1897 which reported

The view of Droitwich obtained by visitors as their train drew slowly into the town station left much to be desired. A halt, which was adequate for the small industrial town, had no place in an up-and-coming spa. A face lift was imperative and urgent. As a major railway shareholder and a director of one of the Midland companies, Corbett's suggestions carried weight, particularly as he was prepared to purchase and donate land for the necessary extensions. Work began in 1898 and, only a year later, a very different view greeted the newcomer. Spacious platforms, bordered by no less than twelve statues of Roman Gods and Emperors' [two of which survive on the modern Droitwich station] 'led to comfortable waiting and refreshment rooms where passengers could await the smart horse-drawn cabs which would take them to Corbett Hotels. For the less mobile pony-drawn bath chairs were a feature of the Droitwich scene. [9]

As golf was being praised as an aid to good health which also occupied the mind it is no wonder that the course received so many visitors.

Bays Meadow contains Roman remains: in 1847 when excavations for the railway began a building with two mosaic pavements was discovered. In 1927 a Roman house was partly excavated in Bays Meadow; it contained a hypocaust, mosaic pavements and painted wall plaster. Crutch Lane, according to Dr. J. K. St. Joseph, F.S.A., 'marks the line of a road extending sixteen miles northward to Greensforge Camp near Himley and thence towards the Watling Street at Oakengates'. [10]

It appears the Romans were aware of the salt springs and they built a fort at Dodderhill, which was first occupied between 47-70 AD and again in the second century. More Roman material was found in an area south of the River Salwarpe, according to the article quoted above.

It is fascinating to recall that the Romans played a game they called 'paganica' which had some slight resemblance to golf as we know it - to the extent of using a leather cased ball stuffed with feathers. [11] Perhaps we should be celebrating the second millennium of golf at Droitwich!

This would not have concerned George Cawsey too much but he is part of the wider history of the game. He was born near Westward Ho in 1863 and so began his golf career on the second oldest links in England. Only Royal Blackheath is older, but that club no longer plays on its original course.

George and his school mates soon became keen on the game, holding their own tournaments with improvised baffies and niblicks on common land next to the main course where they were caddies, along with J.H. Taylor,

4

a member of the Great Triumvirate and five times winner of the Open Championship.

His first job was in the shipyards near Appledore, but his first love was golf and when he saw an advertisement for a professional's post at Kings Norton Golf Club he applied successfully. [12] He stayed there long enough to help extend the course to eighteen holes before moving to The Worcestershire in 1898, the first year in which he entered the Open. He failed to qualify at Prestwick on that occasion but did better subsequently, finishing ninth in 1903 and sixteenth in 1909. Three of his four sons became professional golfers, while the other went to America and won several notable amateur events. One of them, Ernest, was the professional at Blackwell Golf Club from 1945 until 1963.

George also participated in 'a fine exhibition' at The Earl of Dudley's private nine hole course at Witley Court on 7th February 1902, when the Earl invited ten leading professionals to play there. Unfortunately, snow rather spoiled the match which was won by Harry Vardon, with Hugh Kirkaldy second and David Herd in third place. The Earl's own professional, Andra' Kirkaldy, did not do as well as expected and the best round of the day was recorded by five times Open Champion, James Braid. After a poor first round during which, despite the efforts of the staff to clear the snow from the greens, he suffered from the snow collecting on his ball as he putted. [13] James Braid is important to our history, for it was he who extended our course from nine to eighteen holes in 1924, in conjunction with G. Franks, though little is known of the latter.

Witley Court, Great Witley where in 1902 the Earl of Dudley invited ten leading professionals to play a 36 hole tournament

Left to right: J.H. Taylor, H. Vardon, B. Sayers, W. Auchterlonie, A. Kirkaldy, W. Fernie, J. Braid, G.H. Cawsey, A. Herd (Open Champion 1902), J. White

5

Dignitaries and members of local clubs were invited to watch the tournament so it seems reasonable to suppose Droitwich Golf Club was represented among the spectators. It is unlikely that there has ever been such a wealth of golfing talent so close to Droitwich Golf Club. Sadly the course at Witley no longer exists.

The committee of the day were also aware that professional assistance was required for the teaching of the game, for *The Droitwich Guardian* reported on 29th March, 1897, that 'The Droitwich Club have engaged a professional, who will commence instruction on Monday next for the term of a month'. His responsibilities would undoubtedly have included the care of the course, which was the normal practice at that time.

Who, then, were the members of this far-sighted committee which had wasted no time in securing the services of George Cawsey and the unnamed professional?

DR. HARRY SHIRLEY JONES

Dr. Harry Shirley Jones, M.R.C.P.S., L.R.C.P. was born in 1860 and died on 25th October, 1917 after an illness of nearly five years. When forced by this malady to withdraw from public life he was held in a respect that 'found expression in the regret of the whole town.'[14] He had been much missed in the council chamber, where 'his word invariably had weight', to which he was first elected in 1891. He was made an alderman in 1899 and served his second and third terms as mayor in 1902-1903. The son of Mr. John Jones of Stoke Court, Bromsgrove, he was educated at Bromsgrove School and  studied medicine at the University of Birmingham. He graduated as a surgeon in London and came to Droitwich in 1884 where, in partnership with Dr. F. H. Foulds, he built up a large practice. Dr. Foulds also became a member of the golf club, playing off a handicap of eighteen in 1904.

The fact that at least three doctors were prominent at the start of the golf club suggests that Droitwich was developing its reputation as a health spa. It also shows the club to be conforming with the national phenomenon that 'Doctors... appeared frequently as leaders of local sporting organisations not least because of emphasis on recuperative and preventive treatment for which they needed to provide models themselves'.[15]

Dr. Harry Shirley Jones was 'A young man of fine physique and athletic tastes. He identified himself with the local cricket and football teams and played both games with some degree of success'.[16] In 1907 he was chairman of Droitwich Bowling Club and in the following year lent his tennis court for a tournament in connection with the Dodderhill Church Tower Restoration Fund. He was Vicar's Warden at St. Andrew's Church for twelve years and then sidesman for the last six years of his life. He used to travel to Scotland for shooting holidays. His wife, Victoria, and he were prominent conservatives. In spite of all these activities both Dr. and Mrs. Shirley Jones were keen golfers. Harry Shirley Jones himself was captain of the club from 1897-1901 and presented the Shirley Jones Cup in 1898. Victoria Shirley Jones was good enough to be a member of the first Droitwich Ladies' team of which we have a record, a match being played against Worcester Ladies at Worcester on 29th October 1901. The Shirley Jones' were still paying the family subscription of £2.2s.0d. in 1907.

Harry Shirley Jones was regarded as 'a well-known personality, everywhere respected for his probity'. That he was a good doctor is evident from the fact that Dr. Thomas Corbett chose him as his medical adviser.

FRANK HOLYOAKE

Although pride of place has been given to Harry Shirley Jones, chronologically the honour should be Frank Holyoake's. Both families were highly influential in the early days of Droitwich Golf Club. One day their paths crossed on the golf course and it is quite likely they played together often. Early in the century Frank moved to Bromsgrove and joined the golf club there, which he represented in a Bromsgrove v. Droitwich match early in 1905. He drew his individual match with Harry Shirley Jones. We do not know who was the better golfer but we do have knowledge of their handicaps, Frank playing off fourteen in 1900 and Harry Shirley Jones off eighteen in 1909. Another link between the two men was that Frank Holyoake was the first winner of the Shirley Jones Cup in 1899.

Frank Holyoake was born in Droitwich in 1856 into a family of well-known and respected solicitors and when he died at the age of eighty-eight on 21st October, 1944, he was the oldest practising solicitor in Britain.

As early as 1895, Frank Holyoake had presided over a meeting of the Droitwich Improvement Association at which he had mentioned 'the desirability of establishing some golf links in the vicinity of the town'. Having seen how other places were moving successfully in that direction:

It was desirable that facilities be afforded the visitors of playing this most popular game. He did not think they should be able to afford any pecuniary assistance to the scheme, but he thought it desirable that they should form a small committee, and then approach Mr. Corbett and see if something could not be done. He had made inquiries, and had found the initial expenses of forming greens etc., were comparatively small and the compensation for the use of the land trifling... He had received a letter from Major Galton offering some land of his for the purpose - after some discussion, from which it appeared everyone considered the idea of a club a good one, the following were appointed a committee to obtain information and take such steps as they considered necessary, and report to a future meeting: The chairman, the mayor (Councillor Hobson) and Mr.S.J. Tombs. [17]

Alderman John Holyoake, Frank's father, died in July 1897, aged eighty-one, and Frank was made an Alderman to succeed him. John Holyoake was mayor four times and his son was mayor twice, in 1892 and 1893. Frank was an all-round sportsman who played cricket and football. In his younger days Frank was invited to play soccer for England but his principal would not allow him the time off. He was also one of three Holyoakes playing hockey for Droitwich and was president of Droitwich Hockey Club.

Frank was very involved in local community affairs and later in 1895 he presided over another meeting of the Droitwich Improvement Association at which a resolution was passed thanking Mr. Corbett for the new Brine Baths Park.

The Shirley Jones and Holyoake families were typical of the founding families of Droitwich Golf Club. They were active in public service alike in the town and in the club and at this period, when we were experiencing the patronage of the Corbetts, the affairs of town and club were much more closely related than they became later. There are records of at least another two of Frank Holyoake's brothers playing golf for Droitwich. John was singled out for thanks at the A.G.M. of 1903, as a member whose 'services have been invaluable and by whose kind efforts the work of the secretary has been reduced to a minimum'. Later a vote of thanks was accorded to him 'for looking after the ground'. [18] Frank's son , Col. A.V. Holyoake, was town clerk for twenty-three years and wrote *Dear Little Droitwich*, which was published in 1977. Frank's grandson, Lt. A. F. Holyoake, M.C. wrote for John Weston , in 1991:

Frank Holyoake was my grandfather and John Holyoake my great grandfather. John Holyoake lived in a house where the Impney now stands and then moved to St. Andrews House next to the church in Droitwich. Frank Holyoake lived at various addresses in Droitwich before moving with his family to Bromsgrove early this century. Ronald H. Holyoake (uncle) played cricket for Bromsgrove and also for the county. My parents Arthur and Joyce Holyoake were actively involved with the golf club. My mother was handicap secretary in the twenties and thirties.

The ladies play for a trophy called the Holyoake Cup, which was presented in 1932 and was won by Joyce in 1938. She was captain in 1936 and when she gave up that post in the autumn she was elected president, a post she was still holding ten years later when things returned to normal after World War II. At an extraordinary general meeting in 1941, Mrs. Holyoake had agreed to take charge of the ladies challenge trophies.

THOMAS TOWNSEND

Another of the club's 'chief promoters' was Thomas Townsend, who had retired after thirty years as headmaster of King Edwards School, Gem Street, Birmingham, which became K.E.G.S. Aston. He took full advantage of the golf club and was still playing as an old man. The Droitwich Guardian of 14th May 1905 reported: 'he performed a remarkable feat on the links the previous day where he did the eighth hole in one stroke'. The 'previous day' was the day before his eightieth birthday! He died at the age of ninety three.

DR. PERCY AUSTIN RODEN

The club's third 'chief promoter' was Dr. Percy Austin Roden (1859-1932). His father had been mayor of Droitwich five times between 1865 and 1887 and he held that office himself from 1918 until 1920. In 1895 he was medical officer of health in the town. His wife was a leading member of the club's ladies section. The doctor was a lieutenant in the Veteran Volunteers Rifle Shooting team and played cricket for the Droitwich West End Club. He was a freemason and one of the original seven subscribers when Droitwich Golf Club Ltd was established in 1923. During World War I he was commandant of the Red Cross Hospital billeted at Westford House from where his wife launched  an appeal for gifts of tobacco, fruit and vegetables. The Roden family lived at Westford House for a period before the turn of the century.

Mr. S. J. Tombs was the Secretary of the Droitwich Improvement Association and a member of the committee appointed to enquire into the possibilities of a golf club. He was the town clerk for thirty-four years, in succession to his father and retired in 1908. He was a major in the Droitwich Volunteers and won a medal for shooting in 1907, another founder member who was a crack shot. The two Miss Tombs, who played in the ladies' opening match against Worcester, were probably his daughters.

REV. F. D. RICHARDSON

Harry Shirley Jones was succeeded as captain of the club in 1902 by The Rev. F. D. Richardson, the Rector of St. Andrews, where Harry Shirley Jones was Vicar's Warden. The Reverend set a precedent for husbands and wives simultaneously to hold the offices of captains of the club and the ladies section. This has been upheld by Mr. and Mrs L.W. Morgan in 1961, Mr. and

Fete in Droitwich Brine Baths Park 1913

Left to right: Rev. F.D. Richardson, T. Young (Manager of the Covercroft Salt Works and an early member of the Golf Club), Canon Price, Lady Plymouth, Percy Pond (Owner of the Raven Hotel, 8 times mayor and a member of the Golf Club), Mrs Pond, Mrs Richardson (Ladies' Captain 1902-03), Miss Pond

Mrs C.R.J. Harrison in 1986 and Mr. and Mrs R.I. Mayneord in 1993. Kitty Neligan was lady captain from 1955-1957 and when she married Geoff Bill, captain in 1947-8, 1950 and 1958, they shared a few months in office together.

The Rev. Richardson was captain again at least seven times – a club record as far as is known. The only other ordained captain of the club has been the Rev. Marian Talbot, ladies captain in 1991.

There was clearly a strong social network among the town's medical men, the town council, the church and the golf club, of which the freemasons, the volunteers and the cricket club were also part.

When the Richardsons left St. Andrews after twenty-three years, Mrs. Tombs presented Mrs. Richardson with a chippendale tray and Judge Amphlett commented that the Rev. Richardson 'did not require to ask his way to the golf Course and he hoped he would have a similar privilege of recreation in his new sphere'.[19] The Rector's handicap in 1900 was fourteen but he reduced this to nine by 1909. We do not know if he continued to improve but do know that he suffered later from sciatica, for which he undoubtedly consulted Dr. Roden, who had written a thesis on that subject.

JOHN CORBETT

No introduction to the first officers of our club would be complete without reference to our first president, John Corbett, who was elected to that office on 21st November 1896. He was born in the Black Country in 1817 and his full biography has been documented by Barbara Middlemass and Joe Hunt in *John Corbett, Pillar of Salt, 1817-1901*. No one was more influential in Droitwich than John Corbett and Droitwich Golf Club was fortunate to have his support and that of his brother Dr Thomas Corbett who succeeded him as president until he too died in 1906. Their trustees were instrumental in the extension of the course to eighteen holes and the acquisition of West Ford House.

John Corbett had married Ann O'Meara, the daughter of the Irish Ambassador to France and it was for her that he built Chateau Impney. 'He decided to build a house that would equal, if not better, Pakington's magnificent Westwood Park'. [20] Sir John Pakington was the sitting conservative M.P., with whom Corbett shared a great rivalry. Standing as a liberal in the General Election of 1874, Corbett defeated Pakington, having lost to him in the previous election.

Corbett was a great public benefactor; as well as providing land for the golf course, 'to celebrate Queen Victoria's Jubilee, John Corbett had given the town land on which to build its Market hall, plus a substantial donation to the building fund'. [21] The Brine Baths park and the repair of St. Augustine's Church at Dodderhill are but two further examples of his generosity.

It is sad to record that his marriage was less than happy and Ann did not like the splendid chateau he had built for her. None who play on Droitwich golf course can ignore it, however, an ever-present reminder of the club's greatest benefactor. He also planted thousands of trees including the Corsican Pines, known as Park Farm Copse, on the high ground adjacent to the present twelfth green to alleviate the barren outlook from the Chateau.

The pioneering work of these gentlemen did not go unrecognised or unappreciated for on 19th December 1896 the following letter appeared in the *Droitwich Guardian*:

Sir,

Since golf is really coming to Droitwich at last, I may perhaps be allowed to express a hope that the picturesque ground selected for the links will be the scene of many successful meetings. It must be remembered that golf is a game that can only be kept alive by plenty of players and plenty of enthusiasm, as well as by some money. Doubtless the latter will be forthcoming. The difficulty is always to find a sufficient number of active members who take vigorously to the play. It is a game of science and skill, but interesting also to even a poor player. Under the patronage of Mr. Corbett and the influential names as vice-presidents and a good working committee, it ought to be a substantial success. It is to be hoped that the ladies will come forward and play. The visitors will, I am sure, think it a boon, and the hotel keepers should certainly find it in their interest to support the effort. It is acknowledged to be a health-giving pastime, and so far, will not enrich the doctors. They may, however, get many cases of golf fever. As a visitor to Droitwich for many years, and now a resident, I am glad to express my approbation of the effort made to form the club.

H.

11

CHAPTER TWO

Progress

'Peace is a pleasure, peace is a charm
Though great be its measure it never does harm
Peace is a treasure worthy to find
The only real tonic to strengthen the mind
So give up your powders and ointments and pills
A short stay at Droitwich will cure all of your ills.'

(Dr. A.J. Burnside of Glasgow) [22]

THE CLUB developed gradually from small beginnings and one of the joint secretaries, C.W. Price, was thanked, in 1900, for popularising the game among the ladies. By 1905 their numbers had risen from seven to thirteen, while male membership had increased from twenty-one to 'upwards of forty'. Mr. Price was aided in his efforts by Frank W. Sadler, a former headmaster at St. Peter's Boys School in Droitwich. He was a freemason and yet another crack shot and continued as secretary after C.W. Price moved from the town in 1900.

By this time the club had acquired a pavilion which is clearly marked on a map based on the 1901 survey. This was replaced six years later by a building costing £20, [23] which had a history of its own, for in 1925 it was sold for £40 to the cricket club, who had to pay another £40 for its removal and re-erection. Twenty years later it was moved again to be used as a paint store by a local builder, Mr. G.R. Harrison, and it was eventually demolished in the late 1950's.

Although Droitwich Cricket Club did not appear to suffer from the increasing popularity of golf, some cricket clubs in the county did blame the game for a shortage of players.

In 1903 'the club rested on solid foundations , and although membership is still small, the numbers tended steadily to increase'. [24] They continued to rise so that by 1908/9 there were sixty five male members. A comparison with the statistics of the Bromsgrove Golf Club, which started at Breakback in 1894, is illuminating. Bromsgrove's membership was eighty men and twenty ladies. Was it the proximity to the railway and the spa which helped Droitwich to survive the First World War while Bromsgrove ceased to function despite their larger membership?

The club's welcome to visitors, still evident today, was extended further when the salt industry moved to Stoke Prior. This encouraged men like John Corbett to develop the town as a health spa, hence his enhancement of the railway station. Hoteliers sold green fee tickets, with the club's blessing, and three of them were specifically thanked for doing so at the A.G.M. of 1903. [25] Golf had a similar salutary effect on the economy of such towns as Blackpool[26] at a time when good health was uppermost in people's minds. [27]

In 1903 'considerably over one hundred visitors availed themselves of the privileges of the club during the year' [28] for which they paid either 1s.6d. per day or 5s.0d. per week. They could stay at any one of several hotels 'within easy distance of golf links and station', [29] and benefit from the brine baths which were 'unrivalled for rheumatism, etc.' [30]

The course itself was described as 'undulating, enclosed pasture land... the greens are very good and are fenced in'. [31] Golfers of today should remember that in those days golf courses were grazed, usually by sheep, to keep the fairway grass short. Indeed, the club experienced 'most amicable relationships' [32] with the tenant of the farm.

The financial standing of the club at this time was sufficiently sound to permit 'considerable expense to be incurred in the making of bunkers'. [33] On 1st January, 1907, the club's first [34] professional, H. Kennett, took up his duties which included those of 'greensman', succeeding G. Plain in that capacity. It was common at the time for the two posts to be combined. Kennett had come from the Elsham Golf Club [35] in what is now known as Humberside.

One reason for his appointment was 'unauthorised use of the course' and it was hoped the appointment would alleviate this problem.

He commenced his duties on 1st January, 1907. As his wages are small and must be supplemented by profits obtained from the sale of balls etc., by payments for repairs to clubs and tuition fees, the committee hope the members generally will co-operate with them and give him their support. The committee look forward with confidence to the results of this new departure. Visitors to the links will see that another endeavour has been made to cater for them and an increase in the club's funds must result, as there is unfortunately some reason to believe that owing to the absence of any check upon them many visitors of the baser sort in the past have availed themselves of the privileges of the club without making any additions to its funds. [36]

Kennett did not stay long, for in the following year Lindsay G. Ross was appointed professional. As well as being praised for 'painstaking teaching' he also received credit for 'the extended links' being 'in better condition than ever before'. [37]

The extension was the work of George Cawsey, now at The Worcestershire Golf Club in Malvern Wells. He received a fee of £1.5s.0d for this work. He and Ross had tied for second place in the second Midland Professional tournament in 1898 at Ross's own club at the time, Sutton Coldfield. Tom Williamson won with a score of 162 for 36 holes, with Ross and Cawsey one stroke further behind. [38]

Ross's first move from Sutton Coldfield had been to the Braid Hills course in Edinburgh, where it appears he was a caterer. He had come originally from St. Andrews, where watching young Tom Morris and David Strath play for £100 fired his enthusiasm for golf. [39] He stayed at Droitwich until 1910, when he moved to Edgbaston, then to Aberdovey and on to Geneva before returning home to St. Andrews in 1924 where he hoped 'to do all right in the dual capacity of player and coach'. [40]

Despite Lindsay Ross's careful husbandry of the course there was a major drawback: notwithstanding its proximity to hotels and station, it was not easy to find. In 1903 J. Holyoake rescued someone from the Star yard who was looking for the club. He suggested signs should be erected for the benefit of visitors to the links. [41] The matter had not been resolved one year later when a further appeal was made to Dr. Thomas Corbett, 'Could not a much finer site be found for the golf links with a better approach and thus make way for the new workmen's dwellings?' [42]

A lone golfer in 1907 on the Bays Meadow course. Note the fenced green and overgrown fairways

Indeed, the course had not met with universal approval; Lt. Col. Newnham Davies had written of Droitwich Spa in the *Pall Mall Gazette* of 10th September, 1902: 'There are golf links, though the experts shake their heads when they talk of them, and Droitwich is croquet mad'. [43]

Dr. Corbett died in 1907, five years to the day after his brother John. The *Droitwich Guardian* described him 'as always one of the club's most liberal supporters'. [44]

This left the problem of access to the course in the hands of the Corbett Trustees, the town council and the golf club. In 1909 the club's secretary, Mr. J.M. Towers wrote to the council concerning 'the repair of a footpath from The Vines to the golf links'. [45] The Council seems to have acted more promptly than in the past, for:

The surveyor reported that the road leading off the Vines Lane to the level crossing at Bays Meadow had been repaired with ashes, and would be further improved by a coating and rolling with two inch slag, at a total cost of £3. The road leading from Grantham to the first gate in the direction of the golf links and West Ford did not appear to have been repaired with ashes and was at present in a bad state. It was decided to carry out the work as recommended and to ask the Corbett Trustees to bear half the cost. [46]

A further improvement, at the cost of £1.12s.6d, was the provision of horse boots [47] to enable the cutting of the fairways with a gangmower without damage to the ground. This enabled play to continue even in the wettest of summers. In 1902 play had been continuous at Droitwich 'when other links had been unplayable in consequence of the luxuriance of the herbage'. [48] The following year was less satisfactory and a rather wordy and rambling leader in *The Droitwich Guardian* on 4th July was devoted to the subject:

We have good golf links, of course generally a summer recreation, golf has the advantage that while its best time is winter, it lives and thrives all the year. Considering the large number of men and women, young and aged, (the ladies will excuse us hinting that Father Time deals with them) who are to be found devoted to the brassie and the links if not to the caddie, it behoves us to keep our local links in as good a condition as possible for summer play and suitable for the recreation of the visitor. That is what we are told the links were first made for and one of the principal reasons for the founding of the golf club. Visitor golfers have been grumbling lately that the links have been unplayable, a gentleman asserts that a sovereign would put matters right, and that one day's work with a mowing machine would alter the condition of things. The visitors pay for their sport and expect something for their money, and we feel sure that when the matter is put before the committee of the golf club they will rectify matters, and not allow 'excellent golf links' when it appears to an hotel advertisement or a newspaper paragraph in connection with the town to become a delusion and snare.

The slightly deprecating reference to 'the caddie' refers to a statement by Mr. T.F. Culley, who was the proprietor of the Worcestershire Brine Baths Hotel, that 'visitors failed to find competent caddies... lads who didn't know a green from a brassie, met members of competing teams at the station with the offer of *Caddie, Sir?* and secured their bags'.[49]

There is a reference in Professor David Wightman's archives which states that a similar problem was experienced elsewhere by the members, 'few if any (of whom) would have carried their own bags. The club was expected to arrange a supply of young caddies, but finding or grooming suitable lads became a never ending pain. Complaints repeatedly arose about their behaviour. Rules and incentives to discipline them were repeatedly tried. The professional was repeatedly instructed to control them. At first the lads were paid threepence a round, twopence for found balls and wore cap badges... first and second class badges and payments were introduced and members could write their promotion recommendations in a special caddies' book.[50]'

Clearly most of our members and certainly the officers of the club were, broadly speaking, of the professional middle class. Although the subscription was quite low compared with other clubs, it is hard to find mention of anyone whose family status was not that of a teacher, doctor, cleric, business manager, lawyer, hotel proprietor, bank manager or officer. This social mix fitted in with the so-called 'better class of visitor' the club hoped to attract according to the minutes of the A.G.M. of 1903. [51] These were the people who brought patients to the Spa for treatment and so stayed at the Droitwich hotels. It was not only the money but having sufficient leisure and the necessary social *timbre* (underlined by the need for a proposer and seconder when applying for entrance) which restricted the membership of golf clubs.

Over the span of one hundred years the social scene has changed dramatically. In its early days in England, golf was a pursuit of those who had the time and the wherewithal to spare. As has been described, the founding fathers of the club were professional men, with the original benefactors being local men of means. The existence of a golf club was certainly recognised as an asset to Droitwich Spa and it was partly as a means of attracting visitors to the town that it was founded.

Such elitism and exclusivity as may have existed did not persist and during the expansion of the membership particularly after the second world war the club opened its doors to a wide cross-section of the community.

The same might be said of Droitwich itself, which has changed in character from a health spa to a dormitory town for Birmingham overspill and is now perhaps regaining an identity as a balanced community with a substantial complement of light industry and more than its share of activity in the growth professions of the late twentieth century. The bulk of the club membership hails from the Droitwich and Bromsgrove areas and in this respect the affinity between club and town has been maintained - they have grown up together.

The social make-up of the club in its early years also influenced a very important issue of national concern among the golfing classes - Sunday play.

Droitwich Golf Club had established itself as an amenity for visitors as well as a means of recreation for its middle-class membership of less than a hundred. Many held strong views about the issue of Sunday play and the debate must have been lively. The club was divided between those who had sufficient leisure to play as often as they wished during the week and those who wished to emphasise the attractiveness of Sunday golf for visitors.

In 1907 'No Sunday Play' was the order of the day but this must have been changed before 1911, because at the 1911 AGM it was reported 'A resolution will be moved by the Rev. F.D. Richardson that the old rule with regard to play not being allowed on Sundays be re-instated'. This was passed by 11 votes to 8, prompting John Holyoake to write to the *Droitwich Guardian*, 'I believe the question of Sunday play has excited some little interest in our town'. [52] The move towards Sunday play was widespread and in 1913 *The Golfer's Handbook* listed 436 out of 1,024 clubs in England that allowed Sunday play. Although golf in Scotland was played by a wider cross-section of the community, Sunday play was forbidden on most courses.

The debate raged nation-wide:

Balfour, the Conservative Prime Minister, was a Sunday golfer but Lloyd George, another keen golfer, with his Welsh non-conformist constituency to think of, worried about it... 'The disregard of God's laws which is shown by Sunday golfers may be expected to develop an equally lawless spirit in those whom they teach and encourage to profit by their bad example'. [53]

It was not until 1925 by which time the eighteen hole course was open, that Sunday play was again permitted at Droitwich, when we went the whole hog and allowed Sunday play *with caddies*.

We have very little information about golf at Droitwich during the First World War. Our professional, W. Hodgetts, left in 1915, possibly to join the forces as there is no record of his working at another club. He was succeeded by W. Gregory, who only stayed until 1916.

When there was a proposal to form another regiment of territorials it was suggested they be billeted in Droitwich and there was a need to find a drill ground. Alderman Holyoake suggested the golf links - 'the members of the club being patriotic people' [54] - but the War Office did not take up the suggestion.

Undoubtedly many members served in the war and many died; F.W. Sadler, secretary from 1899-1907, lost a son in action. Major F.A.W. How, captain of the club in 1908 was mentioned in despatches 'for gallant and distinguished service in the field'. [55]

The deaths were also recorded of two founder members, Dr. Harry Shirley Jones in October 1917 and Thomas Townsend a few months later, at the age of ninety three.

Of greater interest to us now, however, was the use made of our future clubhouse during the hostilities. Westford House Red Cross Hospital opened on 28th December 1914 and lady members of our club were prominent in its organisation. Mrs. Ethel How was the matron and quartermaster of the Hospital. She was assisted by Mrs Roden and Miss Tombs, who was acting quartermaster in 1916.

Mrs Roden and Mrs How organised an appeal for gifts of tobacco, fruit and vegetables in January 1915, as the hospital was already full by this time.

The wounded service men were not short of entertainment. In April 1915 they were taken to the Theatre Royal in Birmingham. The following February twenty two of them, the nurses and matron were entertained at Chateau Impney by Mr. and Mrs Mitchell. A male voice choir was formed and gave frequent concerts, such as the one in May 1915, [56] in the open air. The Brine Baths Orchestra visited the hospital and Pound Day was held there on 20th September 1917, when nearly 190 people enjoyed another concert, despite the rain. [57]

During their convalescence the servicemen found ways of passing their time and one of their ventures was the construction of an elaborate stone sign to Westford Hospital painted red, white and blue at the end of Ford Lane. [58]

In June of the same year the worst floods for thirteen years were recorded. Vernon Wall managed to get through them in his trap with supplies for the hospital, but the *Droitwich Guardian* [59] does not say whether he came over the Ford Lane bridge or by Crutch Lane.

Many golf clubs performed similar service during the war and it seems appropriate that Westford House represented Droitwich in the war effort.

CHAPTER THREE

Peace Again

AFTER WORLD War I there were three dominant factors affecting the future of Droitwich Golf Club: firstly, the need to assess the quality of golf offered and to up-grade from a nine to an eighteen hole course; secondly the club was still under the patronage of the Corbett Trust; thirdly, the siting of the original course near the railway station was no longer crucial due to the rising importance of the motor car.

As this last factor influences the first, it will be dealt with first. The Bays Meadow site had been chosen because it was conveniently close to the railway station and the hotels. By the nineteen twenties the railway was beginning to be superseded by road transport. Our predecessors had the vision and ambition to convert the nine hole course into one of eighteen holes and to find something a little more suitable than the pavilion which had served as a clubhouse from the beginning.

Three main reasons for the move from Bays Meadow to Ford Lane were the availability of the land, the attractions of converting Westford House into a modern clubhouse and the growth of road transport as an alternative to the railway. To the Corbett Trustees and Droitwich golfers alike a refurbished Westford House must have been visualised as a very fine club house. As it turned out, the club had moved with the times and had mapped out for itself the possibility of a successful future, in marked contrast to the decline and extinction of a number of clubs in the area.

Westford House was built around about the year 1830 and, with the surrounding land, became the residence of a Mr. Watkyn, member of a well known Worcestershire family of land owners. At some time later alterations have been made to the building to include a stone portico and two bay windows on the ground floor. The house ceased to be a private residence around 1907 and for a few years it became a girls school... (A.V. Brackston's notes).

In addition to that we know, as has been recorded above, that the Roden family lived in the house before the turn of the century and that a Droitwich builder, Mr F. D. Everitt, [60] after a period of residence there left in 1913. [61]

The house also had a tennis court on the site of the present first tee. As it had no well, it appears that it was deliberately built over the spring which still runs in the cellar today. There were two fords in Ford Lane at this time, Upper Ford, the present one by the entrance to the golf club and Lower Ford closer to Crutch Lane, which appears as Crouch Lane on the 1831 Ordnance Survey map. A sandstone bridge was built in 1903 and was replaced by the present one in 1933, [62] after the fords had been merged to follow the River Salwarpe. The same map shows a roadway called Green Hill Lane running to the left of the eleventh fairway, leading over the hill and across the fourth fairway to Egg Hill and through to the Kidderminster Road. It can still be detected in hot dry summers in the depression short of the fourth green. The coming of the railway was most probably the cause of this road falling into disuse.

However, the town itself seems to have forgotten the existence of the course: the local paper in May 1920, [63] refers to local amusements without reference to the golf course and two months later, in the same journal 'Interested' describes the local beauty spots without mentioning the links. Worse was to come in August when a series of six articles on the town's institutions mentioned the tennis club but again ignored the golf club.

The last photograph of the golf pavilion in Bays Meadow

October 1922, Left to right:- George Gandy, Mr Tolley, Mr J. Elvins (runner-up), Mr Edward Wilson (joint honorary secretary), Mr Golding holding the Captain's Cup (the oldest trophy still played for and now known as the Shirley Jones), Walter Colley, Tom Bourne

Fortunately the trustees came to the rescue again, publishing a directory in which it was stated: 'There are good golf links pleasantly situated within ten minutes walk of the Brine Baths and Hotels. The nine hole course has been considerably extended and improved and a scheme is maturing for converting it into an excellent eighteen hole course'. Perhaps the picture was not as rosy as that painted, for the club was still without a professional until 1921, when F. Hartland was appointed. No matches were reported having been played until the AGM of 1923 and it is clear that some of the competitions had lapsed. [64]

The apparent doldrums at the golf club would have been more explicable if extreme post-war fatigue and deadliness had prevailed in the town generally, but this was not the case. A meeting was set up in the Town Hall to discuss the setting up of an athletics club and two well-known golfers, F.A.W. How and E.R. Fabricius, were present. [65] Moreover, two other of our leading golfers were also active. Dr. P.A. Roden and Alderman Holyoake were serving on a committee that was to press complaints against the Corbett Trustees, who, they claimed, were largely to be blamed for 'the stagnation in Droitwich' for thirty years, this despite the trustees' scheme which might have disarmed such criticism.

At the AGM of 1921 [66] Edward Wilson and Percy Lyde were elected to replace J.M. Towers who had been moved to Chepstow by his employers, Lloyds Bank. His resignation was received with regret. The meeting also decided to 'augment the subscription list and improve the condition of the links'.

The next year's AGM [67] was well attended, but the accounts showed a deficit of £18.5s.8d. due to some 'heavy unusual expenditure' which was not specified. After considerable discussion the subscriptions were doubled, the gentlemen's to £2.2s.0d. and the ladies' to £1.1s.0d. This is possibly the only time in the club's history that subscriptions have been doubled. It was suggested that the club approach the townspeople who derived benefit from visitors to the town to assist the club by giving their support in the coming year. Lord Doverdale was invited to remain the club's president.

At the following year's AGM it was [68] reported that the club had played fourteen matches, winning six, losing seven and halving one, so it seems the club was showing more signs of life and was beginning to look forward to the planned developments. In November 1923, Lord Cobham laid the first sod of the 18 hole course.

The *Droitwich Guardian* [69] reported:

On Tuesday an extensive programme had been arranged for the laying of the first sod on the home green of the extended eighteen hole golf course. The weather unfortunately upset the arrangements, but it did not stop a considerable number journeying to West Ford to see Lord

Cobham perform the ceremony of laying the first sod. Many were also interested in the alterations taking place in the house, which is to be used as headquarters. After a brief ceremony all were glad to hurry back to the Salters Hall, to and from which motors had been provided by the Corbett Trustees, and here they were accorded a warm welcome.

Droitwich having unfortunately lost its staple trade, it behoves everyone to do what they can to foster the town as a health resort. The brine baths are sufficient for the crippled visitors but others find the town very dull, and so it is to remedy this that the Corbett Trustees are doing all they can to provide a livelier Droitwich.

The first scheme to mature is the making of the nine hole golf course into a first class eighteen hole course, with a commodious and well equipped golf house run on modern lines. Other schemes are the reconstruction of the Salters Hall, making it a theatre and cinema in which will be offered, more regularly and frequently than in the past, what are regarded as the amenities of a spa. In addition the Brine Baths Park will be developed, and hard and green tennis courts and a first-class bowling green laid down there.

The Corbett Trustees are bearing the cost of laying out the golf course, of reconstructing the Salters Hall and of laying the tennis courts. The golf club house will be extended by a limited company, in which the trustees are taking £1,000 of shares, and other residents in the locality, chiefly those interested in the present golf club, are taking shares. The premises will be organised on up-to-date lines, and will contain accommodation for residential members. The fees we are told will be moderate and altogether it should be a place where the golfer of moderate means can find very pleasant surroundings in which he can follow his sport with gratification.

Lord Cobham carried out his part of the job in a workmanlike manner with an inscribed spade presented to him by Conways Ltd, the contractors for the new golf course. It was intended that the company should accompany him to Park Farm Copse in order to see the lay out of the new course, but as the weather was so bad, this part of the programme had to be abandoned. The company (approximately 200) returned to the Salters Hall, where they were entertained at a 'thé dansant'.

The mayor, Mr. E. Evans proposed a vote of thanks to Lord Cobham for laying the first sod. He said the new course would be of great advantage to the Borough and he hoped it would help its future development...

Viscount Cobham lays the first sod of the new home green in November 1923 – and the rain came down to wash it in

Mr. Howard Green seconded. He said that he believed Lord Cobham was more at home on the cricket field than on the golf course, but he hoped that they would see him on the new course. He hoped too, that his Lordship would prevail upon Lady Cobham, who was a considerable golfer, to visit the course. The motion was heartily carried.

Lord Cobham, in reply, said they could not have found a more inappropriate man to lay the first sod of the golf course. It was perfectly true, as Mr. Green had said, that he was far more at home hitting a moving ball than missing a stationary one - but he wished most heartily for the success of the golf course. They were taking considerable trouble to make it a really good one. It was going to be 6,000 yards long, the work of construction was started on September 16th and it would be finished in April. It would cost £1,390. They were also going to improve the golf house spending £2,800 on it. That event was the sign and portent that the Trustees of the Corbett Estate were taking some action towards developing the borough. They now saw written up on the station 'Droitwich Spa' and that was the line upon which it had eventually determined that the prosperity of Droitwich must eventually rest .

He continued about the changes in the area and how the salt industry had moved to Stoke, but that they still had to deal with the results of the old salt works in Droitwich.

It was like trying to turn Wigan into Monte Carlo... the opening of the golf course that day was by no means the only activity upon which they had been engaged... In by-gone days by far the most popular thing to do in Droitwich was to curse the Corbett Trustees... but this will now change... Tea and dancing followed the speeches.

Four months later a report [70] described the next stage, a public relations exercise, in which Col. J.C. Milton (secretary of the golf club from 1927-30) showed a party of Midland journalists the new developments. By this time they included a new cricket pitch in Lyttelton Road. They ended their tour at Westford House, where they were told that the new course would be ready by Whitsuntide and that the clubhouse would be served by electricity from Impney. This was provided by a small hydro-electric scheme which used the waters of the River Salwarpe, the generator being housed in Mill Cottage. Droitwich were ahead of the times, for Blackwell golf club did not get electricity until 1937, although they had gas from about 1924, and many farms in the United Kingdom were not converted to electricity until the mid 1950's. [71]

So in 1924, thanks to the Corbett Trustees, Droitwich Golf Club had a very modern amenity as a clubhouse. What of the golf course?

Berrows Worcester Journal in June 1925 [72] promised:

The course will be open on Sundays, and there are promises of ladies' days, special competitions, house dinners and every sort of attraction. There are three challenge cups in existence. It seems very much on the American scale, so far as comforts and the social side are concerned.

The club met the challenge of improving the links by engaging the expertise of James Braid and G. Franks to design the new course and by employing a highly skilled and experienced club professional, William Dean.

Little is known of G. Franks, save that he was the professional at Bradley Hall in Halifax in 1925/26. However, much is known of the life and achievements of James Braid. With Harry Vardon and J.H. Taylor he was one of the 'Great Triumvirate' who dominated British professional golf from 1894 until 1914. His victories were numerous, but outstandingly he won the first of his five Open Championships in 1901. Only Vardon won golf's most coveted trophy more often. Braid represented Scotland eight times against England and played for Great Britain against the U.S.A. in 1921, a forerunner of the Ryder Cup. He was involved in the original design or re-modelling of over 200 golf courses.

No professional ever commanded deeper respect and affection, nor served the game with greater loyalty and dignity. He gained an enduring reputation as a golf course architect, was a founder member of the Professional Golfers' Association and served as professional for forty five years at Walton Heath, where even in his last years, he frequently beat his age. [73]

He died in 1950 in his 81st year.

He was in his prime as a designer in the twenties - 'The Golden Age' of golf architecture - and seems to have impressed with his work at Droitwich, for the Birmingham Post recorded in June, 1925: [74]

Henceforth golfers will find at Droitwich every facility for indulgence in their favourite game under the best conditions. Those who have made the acquaintance of the old nine hole links will rejoice in the greater variety afforded by a course of the regulation eighteen-hole compass. Newcomers will be hard to please if they are not satisfied with the present test of their golfing capabilities. Hilly and picturesque, the course stretches 6,035 yards, and there is nothing monotonous about the holes, which range from the sporting 100 yards eighth to the strenuous proposition of 523 yards at the fifteenth. James Braid, in conjunction with G. Franks, prepared the plans, and considering that the enlargement has been so recently carried through, playing conditions are excellent. With the concomitant of the commodious residential clubhouse, the new course will greatly enhance the attractions of the Worcestershire Spa.

The proximity of the station to the old course would have suited Braid, for he preferred to travel by train as he suffered from motion sickness. He would have spent a day walking the course, then drawn the plan in the train on his way home, sending the plan to the contractor along with details of bunkering, contours required on greens, trees to be felled or retained and the extent of the rough. It is possible Franks' task was to ensure the contractors followed Braid's schedule, as Braid normally used F.G. Hawtree and later John R. Stutt to construct his courses.

One of Braid's characteristics was to make full use of the natural features afforded by the terrain, hence the use of the old marl pit on the second hole and the stand of Corsican Pines on what was then the seventh hole and about which considerable debate was to rage.

24

The club was equally fortunate in its choice of professional/greenkeeper. William Dean was also a good golfer. He was born in 1892 and began his career as assistant professional with the Cambridge University Golf Club. Thereafter he moved to Dore and Totley in Sheffield (1914-17), Clitheroe and District (1920), Morecambe (1921), Criccieth (1922-25) and finally Droitwich where he remained until 1937. One interviewee recalls, 'He was quite a nice fellow. Quite a good golfer - a good swing. He could talk about it learnedly - a great flanneller'. [75]

According to the *Droitwich Guardian* [76] he was only beaten once on level terms by an amateur or professional player and set the course record at 62. He is said to have holed out in one on 'several occasions'. A former member said 'he was a goodish golfer but he was not a personality, he had not got the affability and charm Ben Croydon had'. [77] William Dean wore plus-fours and smoked a pipe. We do not have a full list of his achievements, only that he came third in the Midland Professionals Championship held at Northfield in June 1929 [78] and played in the Open Championship at Princes Club, Sandwich in 1932. [79] In 1937 he and his wife, who was a popular member of the ladies team, moved from Droitwich to Goring Hall Golf Club near Worthing. [80]

Developments at Droitwich Golf Club came to a climax on Saturday, 30th May 1925 when the new course was formally opened. 'Plus Two' in the previous week's issue of *Sport and Play and Wheel Life* anticipated the event, while echoing the views of some of the townspeople:

As a health resort, I have often thought Droitwich has suffered from insufficient booming, but the extension and improvement of the golf course may have the effect of bringing the town more prominently into the limelight. Sufferers from rheumatics and other painful maladies have found the remedial powers very beneficial... footballers and other athletes from all over the country come to Droitwich for training purposes, and it is from fit men particularly that the visitors' fees at the improved links will come... The eighteen holes on the new ground have all been laid with great care, and a sporting test, without undue severity, is furnished. For the formal opening on Saturday next, May 30th, the brothers E.R. and C.A. Whitcombe will be opposed by the amateurs G.N.P. Humphries and A.L. Murray, and the exhibition games should prove highly attractive. Everyone will be anxious to watch the methods of the Whitcombes, who were all the talk in last season's big golf. E. R. was only beaten by a single stroke in the Open Championship at Hoylake by Walter Hagen, the American, and was really unlucky to lose, an unplayable lie in a bunker at the ninth proving his undoing, while his brother was the winner of the £1,000 tournament at Deal. Singles and fourballs will be played.

Reporting on the well patronised event a fortnight later, 'Plus Two' described how the brothers both completed the morning medal round in 76 strokes, 'the display being steady and at times brilliant, an object lesson to most of the onlookers'.

G.N.P. Humphries (Stourbridge) and J.B. Beddard (South Staffs), with an allowance of two holes tackled the professionals in the afternoon and the amateurs put up a very keen fight after losing their advantage at the ninth hole, where the sides were level. Coming home the battle was of the ding-dong order, the Whitcombes in the end finishing one up. Favourable comments were made by all four exponents as to the quality of the course, the general feeling being that it was nicely varied, thoroughly sporting, and in testing qualities not over severe, fair alike to the long and short handicapper. The situation is ideal, turf old and good, and the greens, even at this early stage, are playing remarkably true.

Although the amateur A.L. Murray had been booked to play, Humphries' partner was J.B. Beddard, described by Bernard Darwin as 'a very neat and compact player'. Humphries, whose father and brother were also famous golfers, was captain of Cambridge University Golf Club in 1921 and of Stourbridge Golf Club in 1923. 'A capital golfer' according to Bernard Darwin, Humphries was Worcestershire Amateur Champion in 1926. [81] He set up as a farmer in Bromsgrove with C.H. Proust, his successor as captain at Cambridge. [82]

Jack Beddard played - and won both times - in two internationals against Scotland. He also beat the legendary Dr. William Tweddell of Stourbridge in the sixth round of the English Amateur Championship at Hoylake only six months before Dr. Tweddell won the British Amateur in 1927. He had an impressive record in midland and national events. Later in 1925 he and Humphries were in opposition when Worcestershire played Staffordshire at Blackwell, Beddard being victorious on this occasion. [83]

The opening ceremony and first drive were conducted by Lord Cobham's stand-in, Mr. Jacomb Hood, who managed the Corbett Estates in the Courts, his Lordship being on holiday in France for his health's sake. The ball was retrieved by caddie William Bateman, who received a guinea from the club. The Droitwich Guardian went on to report:

The exhibition match which opened the new 18 hole course, based at Westford House was played on 30th May 1925. The Whitcombe brothers played the leading midland amateurs, G.N.P. Humphries and J.B. Beddard

26

Dr. Malcolm Campbell, on behalf of the directors, proposed a vote of thanks to Mr. Hood. He said they were exceedingly sorry that Lord Cobham was unable to be present, but they hoped he might be a frequent visitor in the future. Mr. Howard L. Green (captain of the club) seconded and congratulated Mr. Hood on his excellent drive.

The vote being heartily accorded, Mr. Hood said the course was a beautiful one and only wanted a little finishing off. Everyone in Droitwich ought to be delighted that it was so handy. Three cheers were given for the club.

The report continued with a lengthy account of the play, which produced

'golf as near perfection as the immature nature of the course permitted. They were only off the fairway when the wind got hold of the ball at the end of its flight. E.R. Whitcombe's approach shots were models of accuracy, and C.A. only failed at one or two holes where he was inclined to hook. A few slips on the heavy green were inevitable. With a 2 at the short third. C. A. Whitcombe averaged 4 for the first five holes, the elder brother being one over. The sixth would be a nightmare to the inexpert, for the line to the well-guarded, saucer-shaped green is over a grove of fir trees, but making light of its difficulties, the couple holed out in 3. To the turn E.R. Whitcombe had taken 37 to his brother's 36. Coming home, both were well up to the pin at the eleventh with their seconds, but required two putts, and at the thirteenth E.R. would have had a 3 if he could have found the hole from a little more than a foot away. The fifteenth, the longest hole on the course, cost him a 6, again through shaky putting, but he ran down a long one at the next. In spite of these blemishes, he did the last nine holes in 39, one stroke under his brother's performance, for a total of 76, which placed the couple on an equality.

The details of the cards are:

E.R. Whitcombe		C.A. Whitcombe	
Out:	5 4 4 4 4 3 5 4 4 = 37	Out:	5 5 2 4 4 3 5 3 5 = 36
In:	5 4 4 4 3 6 5 4 4 = 39......76	In:	4 4 4 5 4 5 5 5 4 = 40......76

In the fourball match, the professionals did not quite reproduce their morning form, and it was not until the tenth hole that they took the lead although their opponents immediately lost the two holes advantage with which they started. It took Humphries and Beddard some time to get their normal length from the tee, the strong wind, no doubt, being a disturbing factor. A three yards putt at the first, which would have given the amateurs a half was more than Beddard could accomplish, and E.R. Whitcombe's accuracy took the second for the brothers in 4. Beddard made amends at the short third by holing from six yards to give the amateurs the lead again in 3 against 4. The next was halved in 3 thanks to a magnificent long putt by Humphries. Another half in 4 followed, but the professionals squared the match at the sixth. This was the unconventional hole where a barrier of fir trees has to be overcome, and none of the quartet acquitted himself with distinction. A 4 by C.A. Whitcombe was the best effort. Fine putting by Humphries decided the seventh hole in favour of the amateurs, but they lost the next where Beddard's putt obstinately refused to go down. The ninth was halved in 4, and the homeward journey started all-square.

Mainly as a result of their superiority on the greens, the brothers Whitcombe stood 3 up at the thirteenth. The next was halved. At the long fifteenth, Humphries was brilliant with his wooden clubs, and was equally dextrous on the green, where he holed a long putt to win in 4. Beddard followed this up by sinking one from fully two yards at the next, leaving the match 1 up with two to go. Halves in 5 and 4 respectively at the last two holes gave the professionals the victory. [84']

'The best ball scores were:

C.A. & E.R. Whitcombe:		G.N.P. Humphries & J.B. Beddard:
Out:	5 4 4 3 4 4 5 3 4 = 36	Out: 6 5 3 3 4 5 4 4 4 = 38
Home:	4 5 3 3 4 5 5 5 4 = 38 ...74	Home: 5 5 4 4 4 4 4 5 4 = 39...77' [85]

The Whitcombes enjoyed many successes as professional golfers and were joined by brother Reg in the 1935 Ryder Cup team, setting a record unlikely ever to be broken. Their story is told by Peter Fry in *The Whitcombes, A Golfing Legend* (Grant & Hobbs 1994) who reveals that Ernest accepted the professional's position at Meyrick Park, Bournemouth, in 1925. This was England's first municipal course and as the brothers 'were in the vanguard of the artisan movement right from their Berrow days', [86] the choice of these two professionals to open the new Droitwich course was a happy one for a club which was destined to broaden its social base.

DROITWICH GOLF CLUB, LIMITED,
WEST FORD, DROITWICH SPA.
PHONE: DROITWICH 74.

....*Competition.*

LENGTH OF COURSE
6035 YDS.

TOTAL BOGEY
78.

Player... Date.....................

No.	Yards	Bogey	Score	H'cap Strokes	Result: Won+ Lost — H'v'd o	No.	Yards	Bogey	Score	H'cap Strokes	Result: Won + Lost — H'v'd o
1	460	5	10	—		10	420	5	10	4	0
2	475	5	10	—		11	375	5	7		
3	160	3	6	+		12	200	4	12		—
4	230	4	7	—		13	345	4	7		+
5	280	4	9	—		14	310	4	8		+
6	140	3	4	+		15	525	5	9		+
7	370	5	9	—		16	465	5			
8	100	3	4			17	460	5			
9	350	5	9	—		18	370	4	9		0
	2565	37					3470	41			

BOGEY.
+ Won
— Lost }Result.
o Halved

.....................Up

.....................Down

Marked by.........................

MEDAL.
Out.....................
In.....................
Total.....................
Handicap.....................
Nett.....................

<----- THE TOTAL WIDTH OF THIS CARD MEASURES 6 INCHES. ----->

OUT OF BOUNDS

Fence on left No.	4	
" "	5	
" "	6X	
" "	8	Penalty
" "	10	from Tee
" "	13	distance
" "	14X	only
" "	15	
Spinney on right No.	16	
Clubhouse Enclosure.		

X Players must not retrieve any Golf Balls at holes marked as above. All players must replace the turf and fill up any marks, etc., made by them in the Bunkers.

Any ball lying on steps at No. 5 may be dropped without penalty. Any ball lying on roadway between Greens No. 7 & No. 10 may be dropped under penalty one stroke.

This is thought to be the course that the Whitcombe brothers played in 1925. If so by 1928 it had been changed. Note the first hole at 460 yards which could surely have only been possible by combining the present first and eleventh holes into one long par five. The eighteenth is obviously the present ninth, but how could three of the last four holes be par fives?

CHAPTER FOUR

Sunshine and Clouds

THINGS SOON settled down at Droitwich after the exhibition opening of 1925. County, regional, national and international golf were far removed from play at Droitwich, which had become something of a bolt-hole, as witnessed by two writers, one of whom centred his career on writing about golf, the other using golf in a number of his most successful stories. As well as immortalising Bertie Wooster and Jeeves, P.G. Wodehouse wrote a number of classic volumes of golfing stories. Although his handicap was eighteen or higher, he was very keen on and knowledgeable about the game and held the opinion that the 'rabbit' enjoyed the game as much, if not more than, the scratch golfer. In his biography it is recorded that in 1920 'he popped to Droitwich to brood' [87] in reality he was trying to avoid an unwelcome visitor, rather like Bertie Wooster and his aunt.

He apparently returned in about 1924: 'They took the train at Paddington and settled at the Impney Hotel outside what is, outside A.E. Housman's Clun, the quietest place under the sun, Droitwich in Worcestershire where the Brine Baths are'.

Another famous writer must have read 'Bring on the girls' from which the last quotation came, for he too, described Droitwich as 'one of the quietest places under the sun'. Bernard Darwin, our most celebrated golf writer, used Droitwich for rest and recuperation as well as work. He used to stay at Ayrshire House in Corbett Avenue and he praised its library, where he read a lot of new books. In the final volume of his autobiography, *The World that Fred Made*, he called Droitwich 'a friend of fifteen years' standing.' He used to come annually for three weeks, finding 'some wonderfully soothing and restful quality, one lives the life of a happy slug and feels wonderfully refreshed by it'. He described Droitwich as 'an agreeably sleepy hollow'. [88] Darwin also included an essay on 'The Cure' in his 1948 collection, *Every Idle Dream*, in which he describes the delights of the brine baths. Strangely, though, he does not name Droitwich, disguising it as 'Pharphar', but identification is clear from his accounts

The residential Clubhouse c 1927. The professionals shop can just be seen through the trees on the left. The greenkeeper using the mower is probably T.E. Sheppard

1st tee in 1927. At that time only the 1st and 18th holes were on the clubhouse side of Crutch Lane.

of trips to other Worcestershire beauty spots to which he gives their proper names.

It is unlikely that he visited the course as his 'cure nearly always comes between two spells of golf, which emphasises its quality of restful contrast'. There was a link with the club, though, for at the Brine Baths Darwin was a patient of Dr. Neligan, husband of Kate and father of Kitty. Although it cannot be proved it is more likely that Wodehouse might have ventured onto the course.

The secretary at this time was Col. J. C. Milton, who lived at Upper Ford in Ford Lane, which became, until recently, The Lovett School. Towards the end of his time in office, in 1929, a coach house was converted into a caddie shed, which was eventually demolished in the 1980's by David Rea and his staff to make room for the present car park.

In the late twenties the caddies were paid 2s.0d or 2s.6d per round, which they proceeded to gamble at cards in their shed between engagements. Their route from Droitwich to the course was either down Ford Lane or via the Vines, across the railway lines by Bays Meadow, near the present 13th green, over Green Hill then via Crutch Lane to Westford House. Between twenty and thirty caddies would arrive on weekdays, evenings and holidays, some coming at 8.30 a.m. and staying all day. They would go looking for balls, which they later sold if not required to caddy that day; if required they often did two rounds a day, all year round. They had their own competition and also a mixed match against their employers, whom they usually defeated.

The caddies included Cyril Duggan, his older brother Jim and Ernie Brown who later became a professional footballer for Birmingham City. In 1933 the journalist Harry Bush and cartoonist Norman Edwards of the *Birmingham Gazette* were assigned to cover the course for a series of articles 'Around Midland Golf Courses'. Norman Edwards, eighty nine at the time of writing writes: 'Harry Bush and I both played golf and were honoured to play and feature on every course in the West Midlands. It was a most enjoyable task. I still have a vivid memory of the blind hole over the trees at the seventh.* Yes I can remember the pro. William Dean with his emphasis on the perfect swing'. The article is reproduced on the next page with the cartoons.

The seventh hole was to feature later in an article by J.G. Pelley, the editor of *The London Rotarian*[89] who was a regular visitor later in the thirties. By 1937 William Dean had been succeeded by Ben Croydon, Pelley recalls:

For the jaded City man a round of golf, followed by a dip in the brine bath, is an excellent tonic. We speak from experience. We revelled in several games with the genial secretary, Mr. 'Hookey' Walker (who is in every sense a great fellow, famous also in cricket and football circles), and more games with Ben Croydon, the robust and accommodating professional, and Mr. H. Bradley, the efficient steward, spares no pains to ensure perfect service to all.

The hole over the trees was the sixth hole when the Whitcombe Brothers played the exhibition match in 1925.

Around Midland Golf Courses – No 12

DROITWICH: NOT A COURSE FOR THE "TIGER," BUT –

Picturesque, Sporting — in Fact, Irresistible for the Average Player

By
W. H. BUSH:
Sketches by
NORMAN EDWARDS

THERE is one grave disadvantage in being a tiger at golf: inevitably one develops the golfing mind, and the golfing mind is one with a single outlook.

The golfing tiger never really cares where he plays golf so long as the course is of a quality designed to constitute the stiffest possible test of his prowess. Give him the choice between a championship course set in a barren waste, and an ordinary course in the most beautiful county in England, and he will choose the championship course in the barren waste every time.

The golfing tiger never cares about scenery because he never really sees it. His eyes merely register impressions of patches of fairway where he desires that his drive shall finish; of bunkers it is necessary to avoid; of greens he wishes to attain. And in between shots, he just tramps along, hands in pockets and head down, blind to everything except a mental picture of the next shot.

The most graceful church spire in the distance is nothing to him but something the Ecclesiastical Commissioners have put there to mark the exact line for the long blind second shot over the hillock; the most ancient and beautiful old oak is to him nothing but a hazard; and the most glorious prospect is nothing but an annoying temptation calculated to take his mind off the game.

Only when the tiger is back in the clubhouse, glass in hand, may he remark favourably on the view. Even then, however, the chances are that he will most likely be visualising the beauty of his mashie pitch to the ninth.

All this being more or less true, it will be apparent to all those that know the Droitwich course that it is not one for the tiger. For one thing there are many other courses in the Midlands which offer stiffer tests of golf – real golf, for another thing, the course in an environment so attractive scenically that the compelling beauty of the prospect is certain to break through the concentration necessary to the better golf.

No, Droitwich is no course for the golfing tiger. But the average golfer – the handicap man who plays the game for the sake of recreation, or of health or both, and who prefers a course that is picturesque to a better one that is not – the average golfer can usually be relied upon to find Droitwich irresistible.

Situated three-quarters of a mile from Droitwich Spa on the north side, the course is laid out on land typical of well-wooded Worcestershire at its most picturesque.

Belts of ancient trees almost surround it; here and there it is splashed with golden gorse and purple heather, in the middle rises a hill, crowned with firs, from which can be seen the Malvern, the Abberley and other ranges of hills. From every part of the course there is a view which entrances the eye.

H WALKER,
Secretary.

The Droitwich course is charming. And, while it can never be said to conform to the highest standards of golf architecture, it nevertheless provides for the average golfer a most sporting – even – exciting game.

For Droitwich has not been laid out to test the tiger; it has been constructed to give the average golfer pleasure. And it does so even to the length of flouting some of the cardinal principles of golf course architecture.

Take, for example, its celebrated seventh hole. It is a short one of 140 yards situated on the very summit of the fir-crowned hill on and about which the course is laid out.

Between the tee and the well-guarded saucer green stands a belt of fir trees. The trees are so thickly placed that it is impossible to see the green. And it is more than ordinarily necessary at this hole that the green *should* be seen, for on the left of it is an out-of-bounds hedge, and on the right the ground falls so steeply away that a slightly cut or pushed-out shot may finish a hundred yards or so from the pin.

Such a hole, of course, breaks the cardinal rule of good golf course architecture – that the approach to the pin should never be blind. From the plus man's point of view it is an absurd hole. Yet I know of no hole in the Midlands which I, personally, have found more exciting to play.

The distance between the tee at this hole and the belt of tall fir trees is only about 15 yards. One is compelled, therefore, to get the ball up very quickly if the course is not to echo with a noise like machine-gun fire as the ball ricochets from trunk to trunk. And the ball must fly straight and true over the guiding arrow painted on one of the tree trunks if it is to attain the green.

This hole, I always think, is typical of the care free open-the-shoulders, give-the-ball-a-bang atmosphere of Droitwich. Most people usually combine with a day's golf at Droitwich a brine bath, which usually makes one feel very fit indeed. One generally goes on to the course, therefore, in a mood to hit – to hit hard – and is in no frame of mind, consequently, to traverse the straight and narrow way a championship course would insist on.

Appreciating this, possibly, the architects of the Droitwich course have left the player plenty of room – even if it is only on the next fairway. They have also restrained themselves rigidly in the matter of bunkers. And – noble intention! – they have placed as many tees as possible on the shoulder of the hill on and about which the course is laid out.

What confidence the average golfer gets from these tees placed high up above the fairways and the greens. How they tempt one to open out the

shoulders. How thrilling it is to watch the ball sailing out and down – a deuce of a shot, and if only it had been straight —!

All of which of course, is not to say that Droitwich does not possess some really fine holes from the high golfing point of view. It does – notably the sixth, which in my opinion, is as fine a drive and mashie pitch hole as one could possibly desire.

The green lies on a shoulder of a hill which gives Droitwich so much of its interest. One drives up the slope of the hill, and, for one's second, one needs a particularly fine mashie shot over ground that still slopes up and up, and over a bunkered bank that guards the green.

To the left of the green the ground slopes steeply away; on the right, it rises just as steeply, clothed in rough.

WILLIAM DEAN – THE DROITWICH 'PRO' – ON THE 'PERFECT SWING'!

William Dean the Droitwich Pro – on The Perfect Swing

(1) Take the club back slowly — slowly ;

(2) Concentrate on bringing the club down with the left and brace the left side as you come through; and

(3) Carry the club head through in the direction of the objective — the point aimed at.

Another quite good hole is the eighth. One drives from the top of the hill on to a fairway which, veering dog-leg fashion, to the left, is cut along the skirt of the eminence.

But for the fact that another fairway runs parallel with this eighth, with the result that the man who errs to the right is not properly punished. This hole would be a really perfect thing.

There are several other holes that the plus men would also respect. But the joy of Droitwich really lies in its setting, its health-giving air, and the fact that the golf it provides is of the carefree quality the average golfer generally prefers to play.

The Birmingham Gazette 20th February 1933

This little tribute is offered to the spontaneous courtesy so readily extended to an unknown, chance visitor. It was as charming as it was unexpected. From the eighth tee the prospect is entrancing. We were told it embraced the counties of Worcester, Gloucester, Hereford, Shropshire and Warwick and the hills of Malvern, Abberley, Anchor Dine, Clee, Clent, Lickey, Tardebigge, Cotswolds, Cleeve and Bredon.

As you stand you forget the terrible seventh, which has to be seen to be believed. Ben Croydon told us that when Sherlock played he declared it inhuman, and recommended its elimination:

The tee is some twenty yards from a belt of pines. There is no way round or through. You have to loft blindly over the wood, avoid the bunkers, the out of bounds fence at the side and back of the green, the sheer fall on the other side and persuade the ball to stick on what looks like a pleasant greensward saucer.

More will be revealed about this notorious hole later in the story. It seems to have been one of Braid's less conventional creations and it is hard to believe that he was unaware of the rate at which pines grow, both upwards and outwards or that he failed to provide an alternative route to the hole.

James Sherlock, the professional who criticised the hole, was well-known and respected throughout the country. He was the professional to the Oxford University Club from 1898 until 1908, then at Stoke Poges from 1908 to 1920, when he moved to Hunstanton, remaining there until 1932. The 1937 edition of the *Golfer's Handbook* states that he was born and bred in Oxford and although 'He never won the Championship, there was one year in which he was probably the most successful professional in the whole country'.

In the 1904 Open James Sherlock was in fourth position after two rounds, which at that time were qualifying rounds. He won the News of the World Matchplay in 1910 and in the same year played in the Midland Match Play Tournament at Olton and appears on a photograph there with Braid, Vardon and Arnaud Massy. Massy was the first overseas player to become Open Champion in 1907 and Michael Hobbs describes him as 'the greatest French golfer ever'. [90]

Hookey Walker, secretary from 1st September 1930 is recalled as being: 'a genuine character of the old school... he looked like a turtle, he had a totally bald head, very brown always and a slightly hooked nose, he looked like a benevolent turtle. His mainstay of life was pink gin and, like Brackie, he had the most beautiful copperplate handwriting. He was a very, very nice chap, enormously popular with everybody and I never heard a word against him.'

Despite the reference to his hooked nose, Hookey Walker's nickname was conferred upon him for his liking for the hook shot at cricket, [91] a game he played well in his youth. Hookey Walker used to like gambling and playing cards, which he did long after closing time with anyone he could persuade to play. He certainly was genial and it is said 'he cared for the needs of the residents.' [92] F.W.E. Sharples, the proprietor of the Raven Hotel, known affectionately as 'The Skipper', when he was captain of the club, used to go from Droitwich every day at noon to see what the secretary was up to. [93]

One of Hookey's activities was to organise his staff into a team which played the club - eight a side.[94] In that team was Alf Woodall the head greenkeeper, who did not hand over to David Rea until 1974. Both David and Ron Wall [95] respected Alf. Ron was chairman of greens for ten years, including eight with Alf.

It has to be said that Hookey Walker was seen differently by young boys. Brian Croydon, son of Ben the professional, who lived at Westford Lodge, was allowed to go as far as the conker tree, but if he went further than that, he was chased away by the secretary. John Baylis, who grew up on the Berry Hill farm adjacent to the golf course, also bears testimony to the regularity with which Hookey Walker patrolled the Bays Meadow end of the course and chased away youngsters like himself, who used to play on the course and look for newts in the pond by the ninth green. John remembers Hookey brandishing a golf club and being the epitome of the irate golfer. John gave up golf for salmon fishing but is now playing again as a five-day member.

Ben Croydon succeeded William Dean as the Droitwich professional in 1937, and he fitted in well with the geniality and efficiency at the club. His obituary notice in the *Bromsgrove, Droitwich and Redditch Weekly Messenger* on 4th November, 1944, said that he:

had enjoyed well-deserved popularity at Droitwich, for he was genial as well as being accomplished in his craft. He had spent his whole life in golf. His father was a greenkeeper at the old Royal Wimbledon course, and as a boy Ben carried for such giants of old as James Braid, J.H. Taylor and Harry Vardon. One of his first jobs was as an assistant at Tooting Bec, and in 1905 he was appointed professional-greenkeeper at Ross-on-Wye. He was there sixteen years and then became professional at Hereford, where he served from 1920-1936. He helped plan the new course at Wormsley and since coming to Droitwich had made several improvements to the West Ford Links. He was a sound player and had holed out in one on eight occasions.'

The specific improvements he made to the course were the re-design of the seventeenth and eighteenth holes, making the seventeenth the present dogleg. Unfortunately, as David Rea recalls, the new green was laid in quicksand and the machinery used to re-lay the green sank into it. A brine stream runs beneath Wychbold church, under the White House at Rashwood, the farmhouse in Ford Lane, the seventeenth green and then on to Vines Lane, where it used to be pumped to the surface. However, Croydon's work was considered a success and in keeping with Braid's philosophy of tough finishing holes.

Ben was not as good a golfer as William Dean, but a much better pro, because he was everything as needed to everybody. He would always make up a four and wouldn't charge for it. He was a big fellow. It is nice when they [the professionals] make a friend of you, particularly if you are very young.[96]

Other improvements made at this time were the clearing out of a plantation at the back of the car park, the conversion of the old coach house into a caddie shed and filling in of pot holes in the drive. *The Droitwich Guardian* of 18th March 1939, noted these and the fact that 'a drinking place had been made for cattle on the new land that had been taken in'.

Part of the course which had opened in 1925 was leased from Lord Doverdale, the owner of Westwood Park. He was president of the club in 1921 and 1922 and probably longer. He lived from 1836 until 1925 and was the first Freeman of the Borough of Glossop. His son Oswald Partington became the second Baron Doverdale. He was born in 1872 and enjoyed an all-round sporting and political career. He was the first captain and treasurer of Glossop and District Golf Club. He served as Liberal M.P. for the High Peak Division of Derbyshire from 1900-1910 and the Shipley Division of Yorkshire from 1915-18. He combined these two interests in 1908 when he won the Parliamentary Handicap. It is not known when he succeeded his father as president of Droitwich Golf Club, but the Ladies' minutes (now unfortunately missing) recalled that at some point in the 1930's he withdrew his annual gift to the club of £10. He was a director of the club, Lord Cobham being chairman of the board.

During the second Lord Doverdale's presidency, in 1933 to be exact, Geoff Bill joined Droitwich Golf Club. Born in Penn in 1916, he played golf from the age of seven and held a scratch handicap for fifteen years. It would have been longer, but in 1951 the new standard scratch handicapping system was introduced which had the effect of increasing everyone's handicap by three shots. He confirmed the friendly reputation of the club at this time. It was not cliquey and 'strangers were welcomed, anybody would play with anybody else'. This was largely due to the influence of Hookey Walker, who lived at the club, which remained residential until the outbreak of the war.

The war was not the only problem, as reference to the chapter on 'The Business Side of Droitwich Golf Club' will show. The Club was at one stage in the hands of the receiver and underwent two changes of name in order to remain in business.

With the coming of the war all competitions ceased, there were few club meetings and, worst of all, part of the course was taken over by the Worcestershire Agricultural Committee for the duration. The field beyond the present thirteenth green, which included holes nine, ten and eleven, was part of the land taken over and was not returned after the war. The ninth was a short hole of 100 yards, the green beneath an oak, which still stands. Cyril Duggan remembers sitting in it and finding golf balls in a hole in the tree. Land to the right of the first fairway was also ploughed up, but thanks to the status of Droitwich as a spa town, a lot of troops were billeted there and their officers used to play golf, so much of the course was spared.

Ben Croydon was a qualified greenkeeper as well as a professional golfer and he cared for the course on weekdays during the war, assisted by Tom, the oldest of six greenkeepers, who was too old to be called up.

There was virtually no petrol for the tractor during the war - it was started on petrol and then ran on paraffin. One member, Charlie Panting, was interviewed by the local constabulary when caught driving to the course, as petrol was not permitted to be used for recreational purposes. Brian Croydon, one of Ben's seven children was allowed to drive the tractor which towed the roller. He was born in 1930 and became a sub-postmaster in South Wales. As a boy he caddied for Lady Doverdale, of whom a side view - face, head and shoulders - was used as an advertisement for Ponds Vanishing Cream.

Ben Croydon used to play in a regular four-ball at the week-end with Harvey Hill, Charlie Panting and Bill Roberts (who was too old for war service). Gordon McDougall, who in peace time played a lot of golf with Geoff Bill, to whom he was second only in the golfer's pecking order of his day, also played frequently during the war. However it was noticeable during the war that the number of golfers playing on their own increased as it was hard to find someone to play with.

On the other side of Crutch Lane were two sheds between the hedge and the present eighth green, so the eighth hole became known as 'the shed hole'. These were a tool shed, where the green staff used to congregate, and a tractor shed. The tool shed was lent as accommodation to the crew of the searchlight battery, when their tented accommodation was flooded. The River Salwarpe, which Brackie remembered as a clear running trout stream in the thirties, used to overflow its banks and the resultant flooding came right up to the back of the clubhouse. One day the wife of the army captain who resided in Westford House found her M.G. Tourer awash as a result. The flooding of the river was curtailed by dredging, the dredgings being dumped on the farm side of the river. Brian Croydon was given rides across the river in the dredger's bucket.

The club had to accept the grazing of sheep on the parts of the course that remained open. They were a nuisance because they preferred the shorter grass on the greens. Councillor T.H. Platts lent the club a fisherman's hut which was put by the first tee and manned by the Home Guard every night. Brian Croydon witnessed a dog-fight between a Spitfire and two Dorniers over the course and a runaway barrage balloon once hung over the clubhouse.

When American troops were billeted in Droitwich, they made use of the course and played in shorts. They did not understand our licensing laws

An unknown golfer putts on the then 18th green in 1936. George Gandy is the caddie

This delightful sporting scene is taken from a booklet published c. 1935 about Droitwich Spa and the treatment of rheumatism. The book emphasises that Droitwich offers the cure and all the facilities for full convalescence

and expected to be served drinks after their round which created difficulties for Mrs Croydon, a trained caterer acting as stewardess after the Bradleys' services had been dispensed with in 1940. One barrel of beer and two bottles of whisky were sold per month. The Croydons occupied the steward's accommodation in the clubhouse at this time. Also in residence in the lodge was Mr. Cornachia, an active club member and manager of the Grand Hotel in Birmingham, seeking a respite from the bombing.

The licence was maintained thanks to George Nosworthy, who was also licensee of the Worcestershire Hotel, where only the two bars were kept open. Ned Baylis, father of John and the late Tich, who farmed Berry Hill used to play with E.R. Fabricius ('Old Fab') and Ralph Hands, who ran the office of Droitwich Spa Ltd., the owners of the club. They also used to shoot hares and partridges on land adjoining the course, have a liquid lunch at the golf club and finish the day at the Worcestershire when the bars opened at 7 p.m. The army captain coached Brian Croydon at cricket on what is now the putting green. Ben, who had been a grenade instructor in the first world war, used to bowl spinning lobs which 'exploded' on landing. In the second war he joined the Home Guard. He sent Brian to Bromsgrove School where he made good use of the coaching, opening the batting for the school when he was sixteen. At the same time he had a provisional golf handicap of 12. This sporting prowess was tragically nipped in the bud in 1946 when Brian contracted poliomyelitis, leaving him paraplegic ever since.

Ben Croydon's assistant from 1937-39, Gordon Gould, went straight into the R.A.F. at the outbreak of war, lying about his age and occupation to be accepted. He flew in the Battle of Britain as a rear gunner. His son Bob became assistant professional at the club from 1968-1974.

CHAPTER FIVE

The Business Side of Droitwich Golf Club

THE CONTROL of the club has passed through many hands during its one hundred years' existence. Its formation in 1897 was entirely due to a determined group of Droitwich gentlemen, all of whom shared an enthusiasm for golf, banding together to form a club to play golf on land which they leased just outside the town at Bays Meadow. Early newspaper reports indicate that from the beginning the club was run in a very business-like way with a committee and officials being appointed at the inaugural meeting. In electing Mr. John Corbett as their president, and leasing ground which belonged to him for their golf course they undoubtedly began a relationship with Droitwich's most prominent citizen, which was to have an influence on the club for many years.

The committee ran the club successfully during its early years, and enjoyed the successive support of John Corbett, Dr. Thomas Corbett, his brother, and thereafter the Corbett Trustees. The first major change in the club's structure came in 1923 with the formation of Droitwich Golf Club Limited, a limited company in which the Corbett Trustees held the majority of shares and local residents also took up a small number.[97] Again the Trustees took an active role in the conversion of the course from a nine hole into a first-class eighteen hole course by bearing the cost of laying out the course. The Limited Company took on the expense of extending the golf club house. This period of influence by the Corbett Trustees ended in 1928 when they sold many of their Droitwich interests, including those in the golf club to Hesketh Estates Limited, a company registered in 1927 to acquire and develop freehold building sites. In 1929 Hesketh Estates acquired the whole of the shares and debentures in Droitwich Development Corporation Limited, a company set up to deal with their Droitwich interests, and the golf club thereby became a part of the Droitwich Development Corporation Ltd..

In 1935, Norbury House (Droitwich) Limited purchased from Hesketh Estates and Droitwich Development Corporation Ltd., all those companies' interests in Droitwich, and it is apparent from letters at that time that the golf club was in some financial difficulties, and that Droitwich Golf Club Limited was by this time in the hands of a receiver and had been for some years. Within the year Droitwich Spa Ltd. had been formed to take over the interests of Norbury House (Droitwich) Limited, and a new beginning was in sight for the golf club. Its new proprietors, Droitwich Spa Ltd., bought out the receiver, paid off the creditors and wound up the old company. As a temporary measure, in order that the formality of the winding up of the old company might be completed, Droitwich Golf Club Ltd. had its name changed to Dodderhill Golf Club Ltd. (*Droitwich Guardian 20/3/1937*) A new company was set up under the name of Droitwich Spa Golf Club Ltd. in which Droitwich Spa Ltd owned all the shares. The cost of re-establishing the golf club to the proprietors of Droitwich Spa Ltd. was £3,500. [98] Although the club was owned entirely by Droitwich Spa Ltd., the proprietors wished the club to be managed entirely by the members themselves through an annually elected Executive Committee. It is clear from reports at this time, that the main reason for the club's financial difficulties had been lack of members - there were only 79 full members in 1937; their new proprietors considered they should aim for 500!

Droitwich Spa Ltd. continued their support through some very lean years, and a prospectus showing property for sale in October 1944 includes West Ford, Dodderhill 'for many years past occupied as the Droitwich Golf Club House'. A handwritten note on the prospectus indicates that the property was withdrawn at £5,400. With renewed enthusiasm and an increased membership after the war, there was some hope that members might be able to purchase the interests of Droitwich Spa Ltd. in the golf club, and that they could then purchase parts of the course on land belonging to Lord Doverdale. However Lord Doverdale died suddenly in Jan. 1949 at the age of 44 and these plans came to nothing.

In May 1949 Droitwich Spa Ltd. suddenly sold their interest in the golf club for £4,200 to two local farmers, Harvey and Roland Oliver, who then within the same conveyance sold on their ownership for a total of £5,450 to a new company set up by Mr. J.R. Hugh Sumner called Droitwich Golf Course Ltd.. It would seem likely that the Olivers saw the opportunity to make a quick profit, but that Droitwich Spa Ltd. needed to sell for financial reasons as their proceeds of £4,200 were paid directly to their bankers. Mr. Sumner was chairman of Droitwich Golf Course Ltd. and members of his family were the Directors.

During all these years from 1897, golf was played on land leased, initially from a tenant of John Corbett's (Mr. T.W. Wall) and subsequently under long leases on land originally owned by Lord Doverdale and Hesketh Estates. It was in March 1955 that the present company, Droitwich Golf and Country Club Ltd., was formed. The new company began slowly and Mr. Hugh Sumner, as president until his death in 1971, continued to have a large influence. However, by 1965 Droitwich Golf and Country Club Ltd., was in a position to purchase its first freehold property, when in March of that year, they purchased from Droitwich Golf Course Ltd. 18.487 acres in the Parish of Dodderhill together with premises thereon, including the clubhouse, for £12,500. This represented over half of the land leased originally from Hesketh Estates. There were restrictions included in the conveyance - 'not to use any part of the property other than as a golf club during the lifetime of Mr. Hugh Sumner', and 'The property is subject to the existing tenancy of Mr. Brackston of a flat, and also the tenancy of Mr. Sumner of the end flat at the Clubhouse for five years or during his lifetime whichever is less'. It was however a huge step forward from the golf club's position thirty years earlier.

A year after Mr. Sumner's death, Droitwich Golf and Country Club Ltd. purchased further land adjoining that described above, from J.B. Sumner and Others under a conveyance dated 12th October 1971 and for the sum of £4,000. This meant that the club now owned all the land and premises bounded by Crutch Lane and Ford Lane which they had previously leased, with the exception of West Ford Lodge and a strip of land that went with the Lodge, both now in the possession of Mr. R.H. Whitehouse. From 1965 the land had been leased by Mr. Whitehouse to Droitwich Golf and Country Club Ltd. and in 1982 under a conveyance dated 22 March Droitwich Golf and Country Club Ltd. purchased from Mr. Whitehouse land fronting to Ford Lane and Crutch Lane for £8,500. This price was the net sum paid after including in the transaction the sale by Droitwich Golf and Country Club Ltd. to Mr. Whitehouse of a small spinney in front of his property which had previously been owned by the golf club. Again the conveyance was subject to a covenant - not to build etc. and no trade other than a golf club on the land purchased from Mr. Whitehouse.

Meanwhile in 1979, under a conveyance dated 10th May, Droitwich Golf and Country Club Ltd. purchased from Scottish Amicable Life Assurance Society - the current owners - 72.097 acres of land on the far side of Crutch Lane for £35,000, the land on which golf has been played for many years under leases dating back at least as far as 1926. A grant of £9,000 from the Sports Council assisted in this purchase. The grant would be returnable if the club were to sell the land. From the last paragraphs it is apparent that, during a period of rapid expansion between 1965 and 1982, Droitwich Golf and Country Club Ltd. were able to purchase all the land and premises which they had been leasing for so long.

43

A.V. Brackston (Brackie), Secretary 1946-72

CHAPTER SIX

Brackie

To a whole generation of Droitwich golfers, one man epitomised all that was best about Droitwich Golf Club and his reputation outshines even that of the genial Hookey Walker. A.V. Brackston - known to everyone as 'Brackie' - was born on 31st January 1901, married in 1927 and died in 1984. At the March 1972 AGM of Droitwich Golf Club he retired after twenty six years of service as honorary secretary.

Thanks to his son John we have details of his life before his arrival at Droitwich. Brackie came from Henley on Thames, where he met his wife while working for the Post Office. Mrs. Brackston came from Newent in Gloucestershire and died in 1953.

At the age of sixteen he went to sea with the Merchant Navy as a radio officer working for the Marconi Company. He travelled widely: he was on the China Coast route for eleven years then served on whaling ships in South Georgia (Antarctica). Some of his best stories related to his whaling experiences. He was then on the North America run and on passenger liners to South America. On one such voyage the Prince of Wales was a passenger. Towards the end of his sea-faring days he worked on the Isle of Man ferry out of Liverpool. Marconi then posted him ashore in 1938/9 as manager at Lowestoft, where the fishing fleets were just being fitted with radio.

In about 1942 he came to work for the B.B.C. at Wychbold, where he worked on shifts as a radio engineer. To gain promotion he took a job as aerials engineer at Woofferton, near Tenbury, for three years. At this time Droitwich Spa Ltd., the owners of the golf club, converted part of the club's dormy accommodation into a private flat which was leased as an independent tenancy. Brackie found himself

'the grateful but somewhat dubious tenant of this flat. Though never having struck a golf ball in his life, one could not resist the attraction of the nineteenth hole beneath him and the greensward around him and so proceeded to find out what this fascinating sport was all about. This he learned the hard way for within a few months he was persuaded to

45

become the honorary secretary representing the club members, and together with other enthusiasts, to face the most traumatic period in the history of any golf club'. [99]

He would return at weekends to his flat. After his stint at Woofferton he returned to Wychbold to take charge of a shift.

Cecil Everton, who was the first treasurer of the newly formed Droitwich Golf and Country Club in 1955 was one of his closest friends. Cecil himself was skilled in radio from his war-time service in the R.A.F. so they talked the same language. He said of Brackie that he was 'a wonderful man. I always enjoyed his company and we had some wonderful golfing holidays together'. These jaunts included North Wales, Scotland, where they played at Gleneagles and the south and west coast of Ireland. 'We got on wonderfully well. His handicap was about fourteen. He played very well and was a very good putter'. [100]

Another testament to his ability is the fact that, with A. Williams, Brackie won the Corbett Bowl in 1951 - the same year that his son John won the Raven Bowl. Brackie was also a member of the 'Mal-de-Mer' club , which is not a Droitwich based club but which draws on Droitwich for members and which plays sport against the locals on the Isles of Scilly every year. The format is golf in the morning and cricket, football and snooker etc. in the afternoon. Brackie ran the golf. He was elected president of the 'Mal-de-Mer' club in the late 70's. About 13 members would make the journey.

Brackie was excellent at encouraging members to join the Droitwich Golf Club and also at welcoming visitors. An example of this latter attribute was Brackie's friendship with Admiral Lord Povey (a Second World War admiral, probably of the Home Fleet), who used to visit Droitwich with his wife. He played golf with Brackie while his wife had treatment. Brackie also enjoyed socialising with the ladies in the clubhouse on ladies' day: he was good at it.

Bill Ross remembered him as 'genuine, hard-working and friendly'. Members who remember him say:

> 'We all loved Brackie - he spoke to everyone'. Les Morgan (House Committee chairman in the mid-50's and captain in 1961) said he was 'the finest fellow you could ever meet - a wonderful man. They used to say it was Brackie's club, not Droitwich Golf Club. Brackie made all the decisions even when I was captain. He was a wonderful secretary. When I was house chairman I was given £30 to decorate the whole place and we got on with it ourselves and there was wonderful camaraderie. Those were very precious years'. He was for years the stand-by bar steward at the club house. It was great to meet Brackie, as invariably you would, when you had completed a testing medal round. He was very good at chatting to the members; he would make them feel that they were not the only golfers to have spoilt a card at the seventeenth. His friendly and pervading influence was one of the reasons why many people kept playing.

After his wife died, Brackie continued to occupy the flat at the club. On his eightieth birthday in 1981 a most successful party was held in the clubhouse.

Brackie researched the history of the club and from his writings we can see the problems he had to face on taking office. He wrote

Even before the war Droitwich Spa Ltd. had shown a somewhat waning interest in the golf club. The war years, coupled with their own diminishing fortunes, resulted in the complete neglect of the club from every aspect. By 1946 both the course and the clubhouse were in an unbelievable state of dilapidation. Little wonder that the membership at that time consisted of about fifty gentlemen and twelve ladies. The nine hole course, fouled by sheep, was being maintained by two aged groundsmen equipped with two hand powered Ransome green mowers which were pushed from green to green. Maintenance of the fairways depended on one set of three antiquated gang mowers drawn by an equally dilapidated tractor. Such sand bunkers that had existed were overgrown and had become completely grassed. The greens, which had received no treatment for about seven years were covered with worm casts which at times literally had to be shovelled up. It must be remembered that the few remaining members had little or no jurisdiction over the club.

Following the death of the professional, Ben Croydon, in 1940 [101] no effort had been made to replace him. His wife had moved into accommodation in the clubhouse and continued on her own as stewardess. The pro's cottage had been let privately during the war and was occupied by a Mr. Cornachia... Without appearing dramatic it is almost impossible to describe the dilapidated state of the clubhouse. The main structure of the building had been neglected, particularly the roof and rain troughs and consequently water had poured down inside the building even to the ground floor. Ceilings and cornices were black with mildew, the plastered walls were crumbling and much of the woodwork was affected by dry rot. The central heating was defunct and had been damaged by frost. The only heating available was from open fireplaces, one in each section of the lounge and one in the dining room, and then only when fuel was available. The floors were covered with worn and pitted linoleum and a tattered square of carpet in the centre section of the lounge. Mrs. Croydon struggled valiantly to provide some semblance of cleanliness and service and this poor lady scrubbed the lounge and dining room floors on her knees.

Conditions continued much the same until 1947, when the management was prevailed upon to appoint a new professional. They were fortunate in engaging the services of Jack Croydon, the son of Ben Croydon and

Mrs. Croydon's step-son, and he and his wife moved to the pro's cottage which had become vacant after the war. Jack's duties included part time work on the course and supervision of the ground staff.

At about this time there was some hope for the future posterity of the club aroused by the plans of a few of the remaining members to purchase the interests of Droitwich Spa Ltd. If successful, it was anticipated that Lord Doverdale would present to the club that part of the course which was on his estate - at that time he was president of Droitwich Golf Club. He had taken a great interest in local affairs having served on Droitwich Town Council and had been mayor of the town. Unfortunately, having suffered ill-health for some time, he suddenly died and these plans for the future of the club came to nought. [102]

The third Lord Doverdale had also assisted in improving railway facilities at Droitwich. He raced at Brooklands, where he was considered 'a daring and skilful driver' and was a vice-president of Worcestershire County Cricket Club.

It appears that it was Lord Doverdale, who frustrated at his ball constantly finding the pine trees on the infamous seventh hole, had a number felled when a violent storm had already done sufficient damage to justify further removals.

Brackie continues:

The death of Lord Doverdale presented new problems for the club. He had no direct heirs apart from his wife who was an American lady and within a year the whole of the estate was sold. Westwood House and its immediate surrounding were sold to a Mr. Harvey Oliver and the main bulk of the estate, comprising ten farms and the golf course were purchased by the trustees of an estate known as the Strathcona Estates. The new owners' interests were controlled by an estate management office in London with a small local office in Hampton Lovett.

Of course Droitwich Spa Ltd., and thus the golf club, still retained its existing lease from that estate. This lease was due to expire in 1955 when it would present further problems for the club.

In 1948 a new manager took over the affairs of Droitwich Spa Ltd., with the object, one would surmise of rationalising the company's deteriorating interests. This he certainly achieved, at least in his own interest and much to the detriment of the golf club. Without prior reference to the members he sold the pro's cottage and the adjoining field (now comprising the tenth hole) to his 'mother' for £1200. Employing the company's work force, he refurbished the cottage and within a few months the property was sold to a Mr. Foss of Worcester for over £3000. This cottage, now known as Westford Lodge, changed ownership twice and eventually became the property of its present owner

Mr. R.H. Whitehouse. Jack Croydon was transferred to accommodation in the clubhouse and soon afterwards the company disposed of the services of Mrs. Croydon senior and Jack, with his wife, became the steward to add to his other duties.

Meanwhile there was considerable improvement in the condition of the nine hole course. Sheep were no longer grazed on the home ground and the professional, with additional assistance from enthusiastic members, had succeeded in providing better facilities on the course. Members subscribed to the purchase of worm killer and fertilisers and also bought their first motorised green mower. The War Agricultural Committee were very slow to return that part of the course which had been commandeered and it was well into the fifties before this became available.

Around January of 1950, the present writer was confronted by the person of Mr. Harvey Oliver, with whom he was already acquainted, and presented with the bombshell information that he, Mr. Oliver, had overnight become the sole owner of Droitwich Golf Club which he had purchased for the sum of £5000. One imagines that this transaction had been contrived over a bottle of scotch in some secluded bar. There is little doubt that, given the opportunity, members could have raised sufficient capital to have purchased the property for themselves. From conversation with Mr. Oliver it appeared that he had some nebulous ideas about disposing with the golf course and turning the club house into a country club. However, within three months he had decided to take a quick profit and the club and its assets were sold to Mr. J.R. Hugh Sumner, J.P. for the sum of £6500. Once again this transaction had been carried out secretly with no opportunity for the members to make a bid for the property.

Because Mr. Hugh Sumner was to become closely associated with the future interests of the golf club and undoubtedly a great benefactor, a few details regarding his background are worthy of note. His father had laid the foundations of what eventually became the proprietary company marketing Typhoo Tea. This was a privately owned company until the late 1950's, when it went public with the Sumner family retaining a major interest. Obviously Hugh Sumner was a very wealthy man and well known and respected throughout the county for his interest in its affairs. He had been chairman of the War Agricultural Committee, chairman of the Worcestershire National Hunt and of many other sporting bodies. Prior to about 1948 he had resided at nearby Rashwood Court but the prospect of the impending M5

THE STORY OF DROITWICH GOLF CLUB 1897-1997

motorway induced him to purchase Rashwood Lodge, which had previously been the residence of Major Kay. This is a fine house at the top of Rashwood Hill overlooking Ford Farm below and the more distant golf course. Hugh Sumner's main interests were in farming and in breeding and racing horses. He had recently bought Ford Farm to add to Rashwood Farm which he already owned.

Much of Mr. Sumner's affairs regarding his estate were handled by Mr. F.R. Hands of Hands and Evans, Estate Agents, and with whom the writer is closely acquainted. From him he learned that Mr. Sumner's immediate intentions were to turn the clubhouse into flats to accommodate some of his staff and to graze the land. To this end the writer was asked to surrender the lease of his flat in the clubhouse as and when suitable alternative accommodation could be offered. Obviously, Droitwich Golf Club was on the verge of extinction and urgent and strenuous efforts were necessary to ensure its survival.

Diplomatic approaches were made to Mr. Sumner appealing to his interest and standing in the community and emphasising the importance of maintaining a golf course as an amenity to Droitwich Spa. Following two or three personal meetings he was persuaded to accept the responsibility of ensuring the continued existence of Droitwich Golf Club. As an act of diplomacy he was invited to become president of the club, an office which he accepted and continued to hold until his death in 1971 - a period of twenty years. Considering that he had no interest whatsoever in golf, Hugh Sumner continued to be an invaluable friend and benefactor to the club until he died.

Mr. Sumner decided that he would retain control of the club and to this end he formed himself into a registered company named Droitwich Golf Course Ltd. with offices at Hands and Evans Estate Office, with himself as chairman and members of his family as directors. The club membership had control of its day to day activities together with a certain amount of control of the staff. These circumstances continued until the end of 1954.

The first noticeable improvement under the new ownership was the immediate repair and re-decoration of the clubhouse. This project alone cost Mr. Sumner £4500 and still left much to be desired. Meanwhile further improvements had been made on the course. It had become possible to bring the present 5th and 9th greens back into play thus providing 14 holes. By playing the present 1st, 2nd, 7th and 8th a second time and finishing on the present 9th one was able to play 18 holes. This arrangement worked quite well with the limited number of members existing at that time. At the same time, with better equipment available and the enthusiastic help of the members, the quality of the course had improved considerably'. [103]

It was left to Roy Chance to point out that no members did more than Brackie, Harvey Hill, Cecil Everton and John Waters [104] to ensure the club's survival . John (1895-1987) and Mary (1898-1993) Waters were Yorkshire people who moved from Chelmsford in Essex in 1946 when John became manager of the Midland Bank. It is unlikely that any couple in the history of our club have done more for the club and both were honorary life members. [105]

The officers elected in 1947 served for two years and the minutes of the AGM of 1949 indicated some of their difficulties: 'Several attempts were made to hold a general meeting in 1948 but arrangements always fell through because it was impossible to guarantee the attendance of representatives from Droitwich Spa Ltd, who were then the owners of the club'. It is therefore understandable that Geoff Bill did not accept the captaincy for a third year, despite being strongly pressed to do so.

The Bromsgrove, Droitwich and Redditch Messenger of 21st May 1949 recorded Geoff's words of welcome to Hugh Sumner as president at this AGM, expressing the belief that 'this meant the dawn of a new era for the club after a black chapter'. Reference to Brackie's own account above suggests that Brackie's memory was sometimes slightly at fault over precise dates.

Brackie mentioned the dilapidation of the club house and many members recall the buckets that used to be strategically placed to catch the drips coming through the dining room ceiling and decorating parties of members including Bill Lamb, John Brackston, Roy Whitehouse and Cecil Everton who tried to improve the look of the place.

Roy Chance was a cheerful and good golfer who played for many years in his unorthodox style in the post-war period until the early nineties, when arthritis forced him to give up the game. Harvey Hill worked for the Collector of Taxes in Worcester and from 1938 until 1971, for the old Droitwich Rural District Council as Rating Officer. His friendship with our professional Len Whiting dated back to 1926 when Len's father, Bill, was professional at The Worcestershire Golf Club. Harvey was a member for about fifty years and treasurer for between fifteen and twenty of them, becoming captain in 1959. He was a left hander with a reputation for knowing the rules of golf. He first played at Tolladine.

Another left-hander who was also treasurer was Cecil Everton, born in Droitwich in 1920. He was introduced to golf by his brother-in-law, John Baylis, when he joined the club in 1950. Cecil remembers that his first subscription was £3.3s for the half year, plus a locker fee of 5s.0d. In the

51

same year he qualified as a chartered accountant and became the first treasurer of the Droitwich Golf and Country Club in 1955. His cousin, Eileen Everton, married Dave Walsh who was captain in 1966 and president in 1979-80. Cecil was one of Brackie's closest friends and still plays very good golf.

Another colourful character who served the club so handsomely during these difficult years was Councillor E.R. Fabricius, about whom Geoff Bill recounted a delightful anecdote.

There was a row of iron railings coming down from the Park Farm Copse to the hedge between what is now the sixth fairway and Park Farm. These were removed during the 40's but the stile by which the

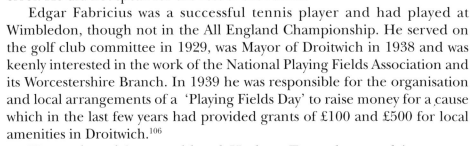

Cecil Everton on the right with John Freeman professional 1954-62

golfers used to cross the railings was too firmly embedded to be removed and remained in situ for many a month. The first time Geoff and E.R. Fabricius were playing the hole after the removal of the railings 'Old Fab', as he was affectionately known, had played the hole badly. He stumped off and climbed the stile as usual even though the obstacle had been removed. It was only the laughter of his playing companions which apprised him of his error. He did not speak for the rest of the round.

Edgar Fabricius was a successful tennis player and had played at Wimbledon, though not in the All England Championship. He served on the golf club committee in 1929, was Mayor of Droitwich in 1938 and was keenly interested in the work of the National Playing Fields Association and its Worcestershire Branch. In 1939 he was responsible for the organisation and local arrangements of a 'Playing Fields Day' to raise money for a cause which in the last few years had provided grants of £100 and £500 for local amenities in Droitwich.[106]

He used to drive an old red Hudson Terraplane and it was not unknown for him to hit the occasional gate-post. One night as he was coming home from the golf club he ran into a gas street lamp. He rang up the maintenance man in the middle of the night and told him to fix it. Because he was chairman of the Gas Company he could get away with things like that.

Fabricius' known activities in 1946 give an indication of his energy: he was captain of the golf club, captain of Droitwich Cricket Club and organising secretary of Droitwich Horse Show and Gymkhana, which was put on in Westwood Park as a part of the town's V-Day celebrations. This did not hinder his involvement in the running of Droitwich Spa Bowling Club. He ran a guest house in the town, called 'Sun Rays',

The building is the old golf pavilion which stood in Bays Meadow. It was sold to the Droitwich cricket club when the golf club moved to Westford House. Seated in cap and pads is E.R. Fabricius, well-known local sportsman and golfer. On his left is the Nawab of Pataudi, famous test cricketer

where the Nawab of Pataudi stayed in 1930/1 while serving his two year residential qualification to play county cricket for Worcestershire.

Edgar Fabricius regularly emptied out the slot machines in his guest house, put the sixpences in a bag and drove the girls who worked for him to the golf club. There he would ask Mrs, Croydon, who was in charge of the bar to serve drinks to the girls until the money ran out.

Old Fab was summed up by one member as 'an extremely kind man, quality tennis player, pretty fair golfer and very kind to young people and what used to be known as a character'. He taught his son Roy and John Baylis the fundamentals of golf.

Roy Chance played a lot of his golf in the company of Bill Ross, who was a benefactor to the club and who initiated the Phoenix Metals Pro-am. Bill's son-in-law Tony Ives also worked for Phoenix Metals and was captain of the club in 1976. It was entertaining to play with Bill and Roy, who always had various side-bets. Roy was twelve years younger than Bill and they were poles apart on the political spectrum, Bill to the left, Roy to the right.

Roy Whitehouse drives off in the 1950's with the old Pro's shop in the back-ground. Bob Harris, who had the chemists shop in Droitwich High Street is on the right

Wide open spaces in February 1961 before the present 10th hole became part of the course. The old Pro's shop can be seen near the 1st tee

These then, were the men, who with Brackie, pulled the club through this difficult time, assisted by the faithful club servants.

Geoff Bill spoke of Jack Croydon as 'a delightful, wonderful, gentle fellow. He was absolutely lovely, very much liked. A remarkably hard bloke to beat at golf, although he was no stylist'.

The Droitwich Guardian printed this resumé of his career on 27th April 1946:

Mr Jack Croydon was born at Ross-on-Wye and entered his father's shop at the Herefordshire Club as apprentice and assistant, where he learnt the art of club-making. This was later supplemented with two and half year's club making with two well-known golf manufacturers, with the result that he is a skilful repairer and can copy any favourite club. He worked on the course getting practical training in green-keeping and laying out of golf courses, becoming an efficient coach and a scratch player. On joining the police force, Mr. Croydon kept in touch with golf and was three times runner-up in the Yorkshire Police Championship, a member of team championship winners and represented Yorkshire Police in a county match against Lancashire. After his father's death (in 1944) he decided to abandon his career in the police force and return to his old love - golf. He has a pleasing technique in the art of coaching which gets very good results and he is steadily returning to first class form in playing the game. Recently he holed in one at the ninth hole at Droitwich, this being the fourth time he has achieved this feat.

His step-brother Brian Croydon [107] tells us a little bit more about Jack. He was one of four children from Ben's first marriage - Ben had seven children in all and when he was faced with a three foot putt while playing for a stake with Herefordshire Golf Club members he was teased 'Remember your wife and children, Ben'. To which he would reply, 'What, all of them?' Jack's wife Laura was a Yorkshire girl and did not want to move to Droitwich. She had absolutely no training for the catering work she undertook in the clubhouse and used to carry boiled eggs into the dining room in her pocket! Sadly, in 1950 Jack suffered a fatal heart attack at the Brine Baths office after shovelling snow at the clubhouse.

Despite all the efforts of these enthusiastic members another crisis arose in the club's history. The minutes of the 1952 AGM make grim reading: The President Hugh Sumner in his address explained the difficulties in seeding the new part of the course and then continued:

Referring to the financial side of the club, he said that though he was most anxious to see the continued existence of Droitwich Golf Club, he did not feel justified in meeting a recurring financial loss, this had amounted to £500 over the past year. Something must be done to make the club solvent. He asked the present meeting to seriously consider a proposition that the membership should take over the financial management of the club on a nominal lease from himself. He felt that if this was done the club could devise additional sources of revenue and achieve financial stability which was not possible under present circumstances.

An investigation committee of five members was appointed to examine the financial position of the club. The club's response to Hugh Sumner's appeal was summarised in this extract from the minutes of the general committee meeting held on 8th August 1952:

The following resolution was adopted, 'That Mr. Hugh Sumner be requested to continue with the management of the club until 31st December 1953 and the club agree to recompense any loss incurred up to an amount, based on a forecast budget, to be arrived at between the membership and the management'... Proposed by Capt. Fabricius and seconded by Mr. Barton... It was further agreed that Mr. Hands should endeavour to arrange an early meeting between Mr. Hugh Sumner and the General Committee.

The club did make some attempt 'to devise additional sources of revenue'. Starting in August 1953 and continuing at least until 17th April 1954 'a free football competition' was run to raise funds. A profit of £314.17s.4d was made over thirty-seven weeks, seventy-five percent of the stakes being returned in prize-money. The venture came to an abrupt halt when the treasurer, Cecil Everton, was summoned to Bromsgrove police station, where it was explained to him by Inspector Faulkner that such a scheme of fund raising was illegal.

Hugh Sumner confessed that he 'knew little of the intricacies of the royal and ancient game' so we must not judge this benefactor of the club too harshly. Although he continued to insist on his grazing rights, he was a sportsman with the interests of sportsmen at heart. Not only was he master or joint master of the Worcestershire Hunt for many years until he stepped down in 1945 but he was also credited with being one of the two originators of the scheme to build and equip a youth sports and recreation centre in New Road, Bromsgrove. [108] When he resigned in 1960 as chairman of the Worcestershire Agricultural Executive Committee it was said of him he was 'well-known for his philanthropy'. He was known, for example to have made two gifts, each of £10,000, to the Royal Agricultural Benevolent Association in 1935 and 1959 . *The Droitwich Guardian* wrote of him on 22nd January 1960, 'he will be missed for his happy gift of invoking co-operation among the members and for his kindly manner and great friendliness.' [109]

While these depressing black financial clouds hung over the club during this period it has to be said that this adversity brought out the best in many club members and that the friendly spirit in the club evident before the war had not been snuffed out. This spirit is still one of our most precious assets.

CHAPTER SEVEN

Two Nines

IMPROVEMENTS CONTINUED to be made to the course during the '60's, including the laying of water to greens, [110] in what was, ironically, the wet summer of 1964. The following year par was set at 70 and SSS at 69; this figure was lowered to 68 in 1968, when the course measured 5,886 yards. The ladies minutes of 24th February 1970 reveal that sheep were still grazing on the course, in accordance with Hugh Sumner's rights and he was still insisting on those rights in October 1970. On the very day that he died in May 1971 the sheep were removed never to return and the electrified fences, which had protected the greens, were also taken away.

This enabled the club to rent the land he had rented from Craven Estates. This land was later sold to the club in 1979 by the Scottish Amicable Life Assurance Society as part of the parcel of 72 acres. The club also bought the 9.1 acres Mr. Sumner had used for grazing, which is now the practice ground, for £4000, the General Committee seizing the opportunity to buy before the land went to auction, at which it might have cost more.

So it was possible in 1971 to propose the building of two loops of nine holes. Messrs Hawtree and Sons Ltd. were called in as Architects. For their fee of £75 they came up with two plans. Plan A envisaged a new hole - the eleventh - from halfway up the hill to a new green in the corner by the hedge above the thirteenth green (the foundations for this green were actually constructed). The twelfth hole would then be played back to the former eighth green or to a new green beyond it (the present twelfth). Hawtree's plan B was preferred and is basically what we now have. Plan B was preferred to plan A because of the expense and work involved in gouging out a huge valley from the eleventh tee, which would also have destroyed the outline of the hill.

Hugh Sumner's death also signified the end of 'patronage' of Droitwich Golf Club and the 'coming of age' of Droitwich Golf and Country Club. Brackie referred to this period as 'the struggling years' and the struggle was finally brought to a close in 1973 when membership numbers were limited

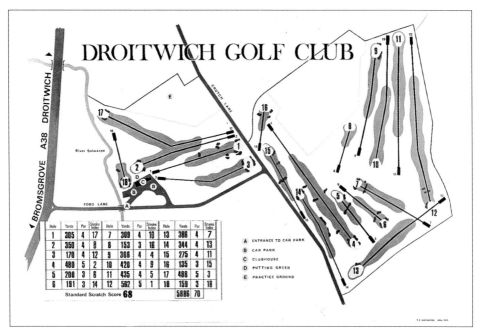

Hole	Yards	Par	Stroke Index	Hole	Yards	Par	Stroke Index	Hole	Yards	Par	Stroke Index
1	305	4	17	7	309	4	10	13	386	4	7
2	350	4	8	8	153	3	16	14	344	4	13
3	170	4	12	9	366	4	4	15	275	4	11
4	480	5	2	10	420	4	9	16	135	3	15
5	200	3	6	11	435	4	5	17	488	5	3
6	191	3	14	12	562	5	1	18	159	3	18

Standard Scratch Score **68**   5886 70

A ENTRANCE TO CAR PARK
B CAR PARK
C CLUBHOUSE
D PUTTING GREEN
E PRACTICE GROUND

The layout in 1975

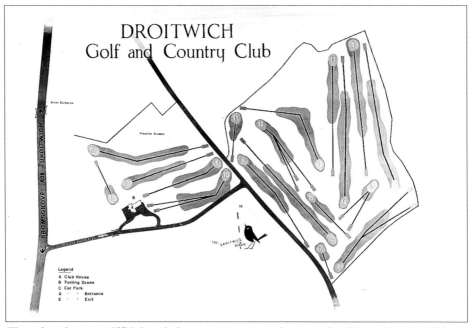

Legend
A Club House
B Putting Green
C Car Park
D - " Entrance
E - " Exit

These plans drawn up 1976 show the layout as it remains today except that the seventh and eighth were not altered.

58

to a quota system. These quotas were: 'full men - 360; full ladies - 60; 5 day men - 100; 5 day ladies - 35. This need to put a ceiling on the number of members was in marked contrast to the needs of earlier years. Many older members will tell you how Brackie would sign you on with a minimum of formality if you had put in a few appearances and paid a couple of green fees.

In 1974 block membership arrangements were made with the R.A.F. at Hartlebury, the Army at Worcester and the Police at Hindlip and Bromsgrove.

This was also the year in which our present head greenkeeper, David Rea, came to the club. A bachelor born in Bromsgrove in 1942, David began his career with Webbs at Wychbold. He has been a member of the British and International Golf Greenkeepers Association for over seventeen years and has attended many courses run by the Sports Turf Research Institute. His main love when not tending our greens is horses, having owned them for hunting and racing them in point-to-point meetings.

His main concern over the twenty-plus years he has been at Droitwich has been to give us the best all the year round playing conditions. He knows better than anyone else the limitations of our course, which has a thin layer of top soil over clay (which quickly churns up) and greens which were nearly all constructed on the clay saucer principle to retain water rather than get rid of it. He is the first to agree that the new machinery now available makes the job much easier. He could not have imagined twenty years ago that he would be programming a computer to control a mechanised pop-up sprinkler system.

Up to this point in the club's history the gentlemen golfers had been content to play their friendly matches and competitions and those who attained low handicaps have been mentioned. It has to be said though, that the general standard of play was not particularly high, so when Peter Handy was selected to play for the county in 1976 this was another small landmark in the club's history. He has also represented Staffordshire and Shropshire and Herefordshire, the last two combining their strengths on the county circuit. In the same year Peter became the first member to win both the Howard Green and the Club Championship and came close to repeating this the following year when he was runner-up in both competitions.

Another outstanding golfer of this period who was sadly overlooked for county selection despite Ray Baldwin's efforts on his behalf, was Roy Green, a 'gentle giant' of six feet four inches. You have only to look at the honours boards to see how skilful a golfer he was. When, sadly, he died young in 1980 [111] the committee authorised the purchase of a seat and plaque in his memory. The seat was stolen in 1993 but has been replaced.

Geoff Bill recalled that 'Roy was a joiner with Nu-Way. He joined the club with Ron Wall. They had both been good tennis players but found the standard of tennis at Droitwich Tennis club low, so they decided to try golf'. Both did well and one of Roy's best rounds was off a handicap of two in the Shirley Jones of 1968. The club has preserved his card, which includes two bogeys, ten pars and six birdies, giving a nett 64 against a par of 70.

On the one occasion of his selection for the county second team in a match against Gloucestershire to be played at Droitwich he refused the honour, as he, and many others felt he was good enough to play in the first team, only the internationals such as Terry Shingler, Michael Lunt and David Kelley being better than Roy. [112]

Roy Chance is recorded as saying 'Roy was honest as the day is long' and John Freeman recalls how on the Sunday following his wedding day in 1955 he duly arrived on the first tee at 8.00 a.m. He had the outlook of a professional and was comfortable with his considerable ability. He was very friendly and unlike many very low handicappers would play with anyone. If he wasn't playing golf he would be looking for balls.

Among his successes were the Corbett Bowl in partnership with Percy Harris in 1960 and the Dick Cup with John Swift in 1972. Roy also had considerable success in mixed golf. Partnering Mrs. Brittain he won the Whitehouse Cup in 1967 and 1970, with a gross score of 71 on the latter occasion, the Amery Cup at Worcester in 1968 and the best gross at Ludlow. In 1970 they also had the best gross score at Enville and the best net at Ludlow. In 1972 they won the Madden Cup and had the best score in the Blackwell and Kidderminster Open Meetings.

Andrew Terry recalls playing Roy in the Howard Green while still a junior and, like all the juniors, he was in awe of Roy because of his size and reputation. The game was played in pouring rain and Andrew recalls being two or three up by the old sixteenth when Roy pulled out his comb, combed his hair and then chipped in for a two and 'destroyed' Andrew. The Roy Green Memorial Trophy was presented to the club by John Swift.

In his chairman's report at the 1979 AGM, Ray Woodhead was able to announce:

1978 will go down in the history of the club as being the year in which negotiations were completed to purchase the freehold of the seventy two acres of the course on the far side of Crutch Lane. Full details of the purchasing and proposed financing thereof were given at the Extraordinary General Meeting held in December, when those present expressed their unanimous approval. We have since been able to agree final terms with the Sports Council whereby we will receive a grant of £9,000 and this has now been accepted on behalf of the club. The purchase is in the hands of the clubs' solicitors and I hope I shall be able to announce at the Annual General Meeting that the contract for the purchase has been duly signed.

The conveyance was duly signed on 10th May 1979. It should be pointed out that had the club access to money and the desire to extend the boundaries of the course we could have bought Park Farm, farm buildings and two paddocks and also an area of land between the present course and the railway line at the same time. What we actually bought cost us £35,000. The total package would have been £140,000. The club owes a great debt of gratitude to Ray Woodhead, a chartered accountant, for guiding us through this development. We became the owners of land we previously leased but did not saddle ourselves with huge amounts of debt as Ray had sorted out for our approval a wise middle course. A further purchase was recorded in 1982 when the tenth hole purchase conveyance was signed on 22nd of March. This land had been leased since 1965.

A communication from Wychavon Council outlines the improvements to course and clubhouse since the second world war. It includes planning permissions for a flat and gentlemen's toilet in 1949, a new professional's shop in 1965, the locker room in 1967, change of use of land to golf course in 1972, re-siting of vehicular access in 1973, extensions to clubhouse and toilets in 1976, rebuilding in 1979 of the professional's shop and a course improvement scheme incorporating landscaping in 1985. Obviously some of these are of more interest than others and it is worth mentioning how the club marked the more important developments.

Although the 1925 opening of the eighteen hole course was the occasion of a grand exhibition match, the initiation of the two nine hole loops in 1977 was marked in a lower key. The Competitions Committee decided:

There should be an all-day medal for the opening of the new holes on Saturday, 27th August, which would be open to all categories with a limit of twenty-four for men and thirty-six for females, the competition would be started by the captain, lady captain, gentleman vice-captain followed by the immediate past captains and the lady vice-captain... It was agreed that the captain should write to Terry Shingler congratulating him on his success in the English Amateur Championship and also asking him if he would be willing to present the prizes.[113]

Unfortunately Mr. Shingler, a member of Blackwell Golf Club was unable to attend due to another engagement.

The captain on this occasion was Warren Davies, who ensured that the event happened when it did as there were good reasons for further delay. The twelfth fairway was too stony and so winter rules were in force there and on the sixteenth. At the conclusion of his round Warren held the course record for all of thirty seconds and Peggy Jones, the ladies' captain, set the ladies' record. As the club had no steward at this time the ladies provided the catering. The lounge extension was opened in the evening with a dance.

After a career in the Merchant Navy, Warren Davies came to Droitwich in 1969. He was elected to the house committee in 1971 and became captain in 1977. He was responsible for producing a new club handbook and it is symptomatic of his devotion to the club that he attended 214 meetings during his year as captain, in addition to playing twenty matches with Chris

61

Thompson. Immediately on giving up his captaincy he reduced his handicap to eleven. He has won the Jubilee Cup and the Raven Bowl. He is on record as saying, 'I have had a life-time of enjoyment at golf, mostly at Droitwich. I have always regarded golf as strictly pleasure and not worked at it; I don't practise at all'. It should also be said that he sees Droitwich Golf Club as basically an artisans' club, and on this question he had differences of opinion with Ray Baldwin who believed we should be looking for a more professional class of member. This, even if it were the preferred policy, is not always so easy when a full quota of members is required to enable the club to function successfully.

Warren agreed to become house chairman again in 1983 when it was realised that no candidate was forthcoming as the AGM approached. He determined to put the club on mains drainage because every summer for years we had to put up with foul smells from the septic tank by the front car park. He took advice from a builder who told him that we needed a rising main to pump the sewage up to Crutch Lane. The engineering requirements (including the 'height of the head' which turned out to be fifty feet) were assessed by John Eddiford, a club member and builder, and pumps were installed. The sewer now goes across the practice ground as a three inch plastic pipe, down Crutch Lane and joins the main drains at the pumps by the bridge over the A38.

The captain in 1983 was Albert Lippett, who made the board for the captain's bell in the lounge, as well as nearly all the honours boards and the Vintage Shield.

Sprinklers were installed to the greens in 1983, maintaining the momentum of course improvements. In the meantime another development had taken place in the administration of the club, following an idea originated by Peter Turton who realised that the duties of the captain were becoming too onerous for one member. It was decided at an E.G.M. on 3rd April, 1981, that the president should be a 'working president' over a two-year period. His duties were:

To weld all the committees together and ensure that each Director/Chairman is doing his job efficiently; i.e. that club administration is being satisfactorily performed. His committee duties will be:

1. To chair the general committee
2. To chair general meetings of the club and company.
3. He will attend finance, house and social meetings if required.
4. He will attend house development meetings
5. He will be an ex officio member of any committee and he may attend any committee meeting if he feels it is in the interest of the club that he do so.

He will liaise with the captain.

The captain's duties were also clearly defined:

His administration duties will be more directed to the playing of golf than has been hitherto and whilst he will be an ex officio member of all committees, his main interest will lie in the handicapping, competition, team selection and the green committees. His committee duties will therefore be:

1. He will remain an ex officio member of all committees
2. He will be deputy chairman of the general committee
3. He will be chairman of the team selection committee
4. He will attend green, handicap, competition meetings as a regular member of such committees.

Social Functions: He will remain as the 'head of the club', that is to say that he will be the senior officer for all presentations at club or open meetings, county or representative golf meetings and prize giving. He will also be head of the annual dinner dance and club functions, although he may in some cases prefer the president to carry out such functions, but this shall be a matter as arranged between the captain and the president. It will also be for the captain to liaise with the president for attending or representing the club at society meetings and such similar circumstances.

The club captain, R.G. (Bob) Tunstall introduced these proposed changes to the members in a letter dated February, 1981, which stated:

Members are reminded that the club has grown considerably to being the second largest in Worcestershire and one of the largest in the midlands. The administration is equivalent to running a fair sized commercial company - we have something like a turnover of eighty members a year.

In creating this administrative structure Droitwich was again ahead of its time for it was not for a few more years that the Royal and Ancient Golf Club of St. Andrews published 'The Way Forward' in which it advocated something similar to the Droitwich pattern. Many of the suggestions originated with Peter Hughes and he was to make further contributions to the successful running of the club.

As well as being captain in 1980, Bob Tunstall was president from 1985-88. Born in 1933, Bob was one of those golfers noticed by Brackie and invited to join in 1964. He was recruited onto the competitions committee by Warren Davies and after a year became the chairman of that committee. Peter Turton, the captain in 1979, asked him to be his vice-captain. During his year as captain, Bob completed the negotiations for the purchase of the land that is now the tenth hole. A popular man who emphasises the depth of friendship in the club, Bob has always been a keen golfer. He was introduced to the game by his brother-in-law and attained a handicap of eight. He has won the Kingsman Cup in partnership with Tony Menneer and the Ansells Cup.

The first working president was Jim Gray, a Glaswegian who moved south to Droitwich in 1970. Born in 1930, he was articled to a firm of chartered accountants in Glasgow but did not qualify until 1959 because of illness and national service in the R.A.F., which was spent at Lytham. His father, taught the ten-year old Jim to play at Strathaven Golf Club where his first handicap was 9, his lowest 5, and, apart from four short weeks in 1994, has always been in single figures. As well as Strathaven Jim has been or is a member of Powfoot, Golspie, Bothwell Castle, Edgbaston and Burnham and Berrow. On moving to Droitwich in 1970, his first priority before finding a house was to find a golf club. He came along to this club, met Brackie, missed his interview because, he claims, Brackie forgot to tell him but was elected anyway. His first impression of the course was that it was 'a mud heap', as he had twice lost his shoes coming down the seventeenth fairway. Since then the club's policy of mole draining has alleviated that problem.

Elected to the Social Committee in his first year of membership, Jim Gray has served on every committee except the greens. For many years Jim was asked to be captain but always refused on the grounds that the span of tasks and responsibilities of the captain as defined at that time were too demanding for any employed person to undertake. It was he who promoted Peter Turton's original idea that the captain's job should be made less onerous by giving executive responsibilities to the president and calling him chairman. The change took place while Jim was in office as president and then chairman in 1981-83. He then became captain in 1984. On the night of his captain's day a piper from the Police Band piped in a haggis cooked by Jim's wife Sylvia.

Jim has won many open and club events, including the Howard Green Cup in 1981 and he has had three holes in one. He has played in the Bob Hope Classic at Moor Park with his employer, Tony Phillips of E.C. Osborne and Co. Seve Ballesteros, Bob Hope himself and Gerald Ford ex-president of the U.S.A., were also competing. Jim has a vivid recollection of the presence of the ex-president who was hardly visible as he was perpetually surrounded by a posse of large pistol-packing security men.

Jim Gray has also made another important contribution to both Droitwich and Worcestershire golf, for in the mid-seventies he took over the running of the Junior Section from Ray Baldwin. In 1985 he became the joint Junior Chairman of the Worcestershire Union of Golf Clubs, looking after the boys' and colts' teams with his friend, John Scott. John returned to Scotland and Jim assumed the main responsibility. In 1986, having come first out of the ten midland counties to qualify for the final round robin knockout, they led the county boys to victory in the first English Boys County Championship at Sandy Lodge. A magnificent achievement for all concerned and by implication, for Droitwich Golf Club. John Bickerton Jnr. was a member of this victorious team.

64

Jim finally retired from his position in 1992 and the following year he was elected a county vice-president. Droitwich boys have continued to represent the county to good effect since Jim's time in charge.

Jim is a member of the British Golf Collectors' Society, specialising in old postcards of golf courses, supplemented by his own photographs of the scenes they show today. Jim is also an ardent golf philatelist. He has been a member of the 'Mal-de-Mer club' for many years.

It had been decided that the club captain for the centenary year should be elected by a vote of the members at an extra-ordinary general meeting of the club. Jim was one of the two members proposed and such was the support for both candidates that it took three re-counts to establish a result, Jim losing out by the narrowest of margins on this occasion.

Following Brackie's retirement in 1972 H.E. Stevenson was appointed secretary but his entry into the world of golf management was relatively short lived as he left only a few months after his appointment, in part because of the loss of his wife.

He, in turn, was succeeded by Ray Baldwin who came to Droitwich from Harborne Golf Club with considerable experience of committee work and a handicap of two. He had started playing golf when osteomilitis cut short his rugby career. Within eight months he had attained a handicap of eight, often playing as many as forty one holes in a day on Sundays. As secretary of Droitwich he helped the club become more integrated in Worcestershire County Golf, which he still serves as development officer and vice-president.

Ray was very conscientious in maintaining standards - on one occasion he drove his car to the far corner of the course to catch and reprimand players who had repeatedly cut in front of other playing members. Ray felt that much of his work was behind the scenes and in the counselling of new committee members and officers of the club. He enjoyed his work although not all his suggestions won approval, as the greens committee minutes of 17th August 1981, show:

The secretary's plan for the practice ground was discussed. Whilst it was agreed that a programme of improvement was needed, it was felt that the plan was too ambitious for the following reasons. The area available was too small. It could be dangerous if congested with members (if enough members were interested in playing a pitch and putt course when an eighteen hole was available). In order to create a worthwhile job, much work and money would be required. Water would be required. There could be possible neglect of work on the main course.

During Ray Baldwin's years of office Droitwich began to figure on the list of Worcestershire County venues. He was also a keen snooker player and in his retirement has been a leading light in the bridge club. The club undoubtedly benefited from having a secretary who was very active and well

Ray Baldwin, secretary 1972-87 and now a life member

connected in the wider world of golf. Droitwich Golf Club would never again be the quiet backwater it had been before Ray came.

Currently Ray is on the structures committee of the English Golf Union, one of five looking into the rules and constitution. In addition to being an honorary life member of our club, Ray is a past captain of Warwickshire and Midland Counties, vice-president of Warwickshire Union of Golf clubs as well as Worcestershire and co-founder of the Midland Junior Golfing Society. He has also been secretary of many golfing bodies.

Ray was still in office when Air Commodore Peter Hughes succeeded Jim Gray as our chief executive. After distinguished war service in the R.A.F. which included a spell in Stalag Luft III he was able to bring his organisational ability to Droitwich Golf Club, where he first served on the general committee. As chief executive he organised the general committee in a very business like way. Those who served knew where their responsibilities and loyalties lay. Proper preparations for meetings were insisted upon so that they would be as short as possible. They were to be used for the purpose of policy making and not for the mere passing of information. His five page document 'Status and Responsibilities of Directors' is a model of clarity and

Droitwich team at the Worcestershire Golf Club, Malvern c. 1972 Left to right Back row: Norman Cox, Robert Coe, John Barton, Jim Gray, Terry Tansley, Jim Struthers Front row: Gary Reynolds, Eric Court, Colin Brade, Peter Pessol, Jim Troth

helped to reinforce in the club traditions of service, selflessness and sound working methods.

A perennial problem of Droitwich Golf Club has been how we maintain Westford House. In Peter Hughes' time a comprehensive development scheme was hammered out and passed by all the appropriate bodies of the club. Two pages of A4 entitled 'Working notes to the club house development plan 1985' give some idea of the hard work and attention to detail that went into this effort.

Jim Struthers joined the club in 1972 and was much involved when the course was being rearranged into two loops of nine holes. He became captain in 1985 and remembers the thankless task he carried through of getting

Peter Hughes, Chairman of the club from 1983-85 at the Phoenix Metals Pro-Am in the late 1970's. On the left is Brackie who was acting as starter

67

the membership to accept a very substantial but necessary increase in subscriptions. Jim was Club Champion three times, his lowest handicap being four. He also won the Kings Norton Gold Cup.

Another prominent member who greatly assisted the development of the club during this period was Barrie Joule, who first came to Droitwich in 1966 with his wife, Wendy. They had married in 1961 while Barrie was a member of her father's club, Hazel Grove in Stockport, then moved to New Mills Golf Club in the Peak District.

Barrie joined the competitions committee in 1969 and introduced the original Winter League, using the same format as New Mills. He also became a member of the highly successful snooker team of the 1970's. He remembers the 'Queen Street Gang', comprising shopkeepers from Queen Street, running the club with Brackie. These were Dave Walsh, Ron Wall and Keith Harding and Barrie recalls them running the club with a strong hand at a difficult time. He became vice-captain in 1972 to Ivan Bedford, succeeding him the following year. Brackie was beginning to feel the strain of running the club and Ray Baldwin took over as secretary during Barrie's captaincy. The two men did not always agree as Ray felt that more professional men should be invited to join, while Barrie felt the club was primarily an artisans' club.

Having attained his lowest handicap of eight, Barrie Joule had several successes on the course, winning the Corbett Bowl in 1969 with John Clark as well as the Jubilee Cup, the Eric Griffin Trophy and the Kingsman Cup but he regards match play as his forte, rather than stroke play.

Wendy took up the game in the mid-seventies and became a very popular member of the ladies' section. Unfortunately tragedy struck in 1985 when she died of cancer. The Wendy Joule trophy was instituted in her memory and consists of a cup and saucer bearing the St. Andrews insignia which had been given to Wendy by her daughter Alex. This was suitably mounted in a presentation case and is played for each May as a mixed foursome competition enjoyed by as many as sixty members. Barrie generously provides the prizes.

Barrie Joule became chairman of the club in 1988, serving until 1991, during which period the locker rooms were modernised and the lounge was redecorated and refurnished. However plans to re-vamp the east wing of Westford House where it was proposed to provide new locker rooms were put in abeyance, because of major developments proposed for the town.

In 1990/91 Wychavon District Council and Droitwich Town Council published their ten-year plan. Because considerable housing development had taken place to the south of Droitwich the town centre was no longer central. Accordingly plans were made to develop building estates to the north of the town. Sometime between November 1990 and March 1991, Bovis approached Mrs. Everitt of Dodderhill Court, and Droitwich Golf Club with a view to buying 60 acres, 31 from the golf club and 29 from Mrs. Everitt. The club would have lost all the land east of Crutch Lane, including Westford House, which would obviously have necessitated building a new clubhouse and replacement holes elsewhere. This development would probably have taken place on land available for purchase on the west side of Crutch Lane.

Whilst these proposals were still under investigation Warren Davies became club chairman, and Geoff Hudspith and Bill Smith were co-opted to form with him a sub committee to negotiate for the club. They presented our policy that we had a perfectly good course and if we could not get exactly what we wanted we would not be interested. Bovis were talking about building 440 houses, with access through land owned by Mrs. Everitt.

Moreover more than 300 Droitwich residents objected to the development plans. There were possibilities that Bovis would be able to mount a successful campaign against the protesters, but with one thing and another, including the re-zoning of land to the south of Droitwich for residential development, the scheme ran into the sand. The recession was beginning to bite and Bovis started to prevaricate and to distinguish between the land that would be developable acreage and land that would just be used for infrastructure. Although this major project came to nought, the depth of consideration involved caused the committee to think more radically in respect of improvements to the facilities and the idea of building new locker rooms was put aside, pending a broader review of the clubhouse requirements.

On completing three years as club chairman Warren was succeeded by Geoff Hudspith. Geoff joined the club in 1977 and soon became involved with the C team which he captained for several years. Despite the demands of his job in charge of all the service activity at Nu-way he found the time to become closely involved with the running of the club as captain in 1991 and then as chairman from 1994 - a period of much change in the club's affairs. He describes 1992/93 as his 'Sabbatical' year during which he could give more attention to the game of golf, a contention substantiated by his winning the Raven Bowl. Geoff is a great listener and he does not regard any aspect of the club's activities or any of the many golfing sections as less worthy of his attention than any other.

Our centenary captain, Walter Jarvis, was an all round sportsman before deciding as the age of forty approached that golf was the right game to pursue for his future life. Although he was living and working in Stourbridge at the time he joined Droitwich in 1967. He has become progressively more active in supporting the club, serving on the Competitions Committee for some years and doing a great deal of work, either hours at the computer churning through hundreds of cards to produce competition results and adjust handicaps or making the very elegant notice boards in the men's locker room corridor or sitting at a table dishing out cards to competitors. No task seems too small or too large for Walter as long as it is in the interest of the club. In between he manages to be Secretary of the Worcestershire Woodturners Society.

Among the players who have burnished the reputation of Droitwich Golf Club in recent years are Andrew Terry, Simon Braithwaite and David Nevett.

Andrew has won the club championship four times, has been a member of the winning Droitwich Shield team twice and, in the team which has won the Worcestershire Team Championship, the Thompson-James Cup. The son of a schoolteacher who is also an active member of the club, Andrew was invited to join the club by Brackie in 1970 and recalls how Brackie used to make putters and practise with them on the putting green, winning the odd sixpence off Andrew.

He started as a pupil at Droitwich High School in 1975 on the same day that his father began as deputy-headmaster and that same year he won his first trophy - the Shirley Jones Cup. He first won the club championship in 1977.

Simon Braithwaite was the county champion in 1989 and club champion in both 1989 and 1996. He represented the club in the 1995 Champion of Champions Tournament organised by the Birmingham Post and Mail. This was played at the Robin Hood Golf Club and Simon defeated no less a man than Michael Reynard in a play-off. He has played for the Worcestershire 1st and 2nd teams for the last twelve years. Simon has also won other club trophies, such as the stroke play championship and the handicap knock-out.

The third of these recent Droitwich members to represent the county is David Nevett, who is now the Worcestershire second team captain. A member of Droitwich for twenty two years, perhaps David's greatest achievement was winning three major trophies in 1995, the Roy Green, the Howard Green and the Club Championship and coming second in the thirty six hole stroke play competition. He also won the Roy Green Memorial Trophy in 1993 and was captain of our winning Droitwich Salver teams in 1985 and 1990.

Hole	Marker's Score	White Yards	Par	Yellow Yards	Stroke Index	Score A	Score B	Nett Score	W = + L = - H = 0 Points	Red Yards	Par	Stroke Index

COMPETITION Eric Griffin Trophy

DATE 3rd July 94 **TIME** 10.10. **Handicap** **Strokes Rec'd**

Please indicate which tee used.

	PAR	SSS
	70	69

Player A Simon Braithwaite 3.

	PAR	SSS
	70	67

Player B

	PAR	SSS
	70	70

Hole	Marker's Score	White Yards	Par	Yellow Yards	Stroke Index	A	B	Nett Score	Points	Red Yards	Par	Stroke Index
1	4	302	4	278	5	5				290	4	12
2	5	478	5	460	15	5				453	5	8
3	3	185	3	169	9	4				155	3	15
4	5	443	4	408	1	5				376	4	2
5	5	564	5	539	3	4				447	5	6
6	3	383	4	379	7	4				361	4	4
7	4	350	4	334	11	3				337	4	13
8	5	301	4	269	13	3				179	3	10
9	4	334	4	330	17	3				330	4	16
	38	3340	37	3166	OUT	36				2928	36	

PLEASE REPLACE DIVOTS & REPAIR PITCH MARKS

Hole	Marker's Score	White Yards	Par	Yellow Yards	Stroke Index	A	B	Nett Score	Points	Red Yards	Par	Stroke Index
10	4	313	4	297	14	4				286	4	7
11	2	146	3	140	16	3				100	3	18
12	4	382	4	356	6	3				364	4	1
13	5	370	4	362	8	4				329	4	5
14	7	417	4	397	4	4				357	4	3
15	4	195	3	177	10	2				165	3	9
16	4	290	4	275	18	4				231	4	14
17	4	443	4	433	2	3				426	5	11
18	3	162	3	140	12	2				151	3	17
	37	2718	33	2577	IN	29				2409	34	
	38	3340	37	3166	OUT	36				2928	36	
	75	6058	70	5743	TOTAL	65				5337	70	

ENTRY NUMBER **HANDICAP** 3

NET T 62

Copyright Eagle Promotions Ltd.
01883 344244

Markers Signature

Players Signature

Holes won ....
Holes lost ....
Result ....

Course record of 65 held by Simon Braithwaite and achieved on 3rd July 1994. Due to course changes it superseded the 65's by John Bickerton in 1988 and David Eddiford in 1983

71

CHAPTER EIGHT

The Course

THE FOCAL point of every golf club is its course. But 'a golf course not only gives us something in common with our fellow members, whatever their degree of addiction, but in an unspoken way with those who came before' (Richard Holt). [114] This legacy pre-dates the use of the land as a golf course, for on the way to the second green we encounter a grassed-in marl pit and we have acres of land which have been shaped by the practices of medieval ridge and furrow farming still evident on the second, eighth and seventeenth fairways.

Few courses have survived unchanged since their inception: even the Old Course at St. Andrews has experienced change since it began as twenty two holes using eleven greens 'out and back'.

Droitwich Golf Club is no exception, the course being viewed as a means of attracting visitors as much as an amenity for the members. The original course of nine holes was easily accessible on foot from town and railway station, a major advantage in its original promotion. *The Droitwich Guardian* of November 28th 1896 described the 'links' in Bays Meadow in characteristic phraseology:

Bays Meadow, although perhaps not possessing the hazards which go to make the ideal links, in the shape of furze, water or other obstacles, still possessed difficulties, without which the royal and ancient game is of no account. Cawsey, the Kings Norton expert, is strongly in its favour. The land which will form the links is in front of Dodderhill Court and Hill Court. It is hilly, undulating and from the top picturesque views can be obtained of the Malvern, Abberley, Clee and Shropshire hills. The first teeing ground is fixed near the railway crossing and play will start in a line parallel to the railway to the first green - about half way up the field. The second lies off in the same direction and is near the corner of the field, by the iron railings, and not far from the line. Play will then be made at right angles to the oak tree, under which is a seat near the path where the third green is fixed. Up to this the play will be slightly uphill over undulating lands. From the third to the fourth green the player's motto must be 'Excelsior!' for the drives will have to be to the top of the hill. The play from here will be up and down the hill, finishing at the ninth green, about 150 yards from the crossing.

Cawsey returned in 1907 to extend the course, which was cared for by the professional Lindsay Ross who apparently kept it in fine condition. The need to extend the course to eighteen holes was already recognised but the first World War and diminished interest and opportunities to play golf prevented the extension until the acquisition of Westford House. Finally the first sod of the new course, designed by James Braid, was laid in 1923.

If we follow the 1928 club handbook, we find the first hole is similar to the present first:

The ground rises gently to the green, which should be reached by a driver and a mashie shot. The approach requires judgement for the green is guarded on both sides by bunkers and there is a ridge in front and at the back a hedge.

The second was clearly the present eleventh and was a mashie-niblick shot. The present second was the third hole and of similar length. The tee is on the shoulder of the fir-crowned hill and provides a glorious view of the Lickey Hills. The fairway lies far below... the green is hugged about with pot bunkers. The old marl pit has also to be negotiated and denies the shorter hitters a view of the green for the approach.

The fourth hole is now the fifteenth and measured 160 yards, while the fifth was also a bogey three of 200 yards from an elevated tee, requiring a drive or a strong brassie shot (a brassie was the equivalent to a two wood,

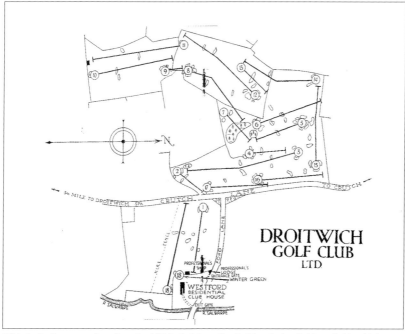

This is the layout taken fom the 1928 club handbook. Note holes 9, 10 and 11 which were in the field to the south of the present thirteenth green

73

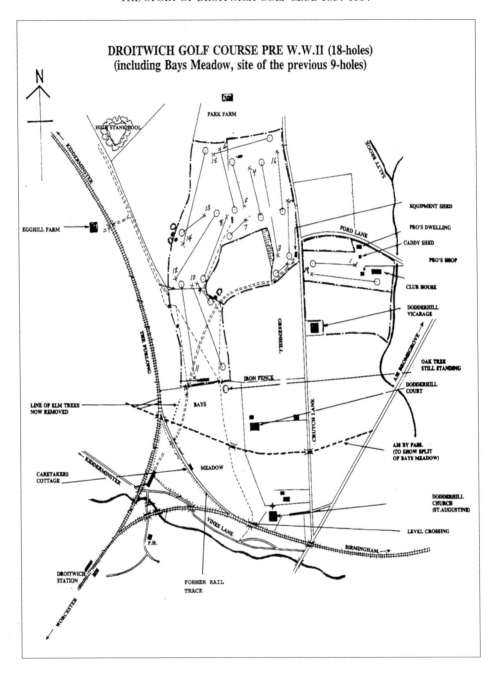

DROITWICH GOLF COURSE PRE W.W.II (18-holes)
(including Bays Meadow, site of the previous 9-holes)

c 1928 (Club Handbook) Bogeys and Lengths of Holes

Hole	Yards	Bogey	Hole	Yards	Bogey
1	275	4	10	350	5
2	110	3	11	420	5
3	475	5	12	375	5
4	160	3	13	200	3
5	200	3	14	345	4
6	280	4	15	310	4
7	140	3	16	340	4
8	370	4	17	210	4
9	100	3	18	350	4
Out	2110	32	Home	2900	38
			Out	2110	32
			Total	5010	70

c 1935 (Club Handbook) Bogeys and Lengths of Holes

Hole	Yards	Bogey	Hole	Yards	Bogey
1	275	4	10	350	4
2	110	3	11	420	5
3	475	5	12	460	5
4	170	3	13	230	4
5	200	3	14	375	4
6	280	4	15	380	4
7	140	3	16	340	4
8	395	4	17	235	4
9	100	3	18	350	4
Out	2145	32	Home	3140	38
			Out	2145	32
			Total	5285	70

now superseded by drivers of increased loft). There were railings marking an out of bounds area on the left and a pond at the back of the green, adjacent to the present third tee.

The golfers then played back up the hill to a par four of 280 yards, the green set on a plateau, flanked by fir trees and rough. This hole was known as 'Spion Kop' or 'The Punchbowl'. Then came the famous - or infamous - seventh, the par three which required the lofted shot over the Corsican pines to the well guarded saucer green. In the years after the second World War these pines though taller were fewer in number and an accurate shot could be played between them to the green.

The eighth hole, now the thirteenth, lay at the base of the ridge 'and the sloping ground invites the driver to one of his best'. This was followed by another short hole of 100 yards to a blind green and would have taken the players towards Bays Meadow, where lay the tenth and eleventh holes. The former, near the old clubhouse, was a bogey five of 350 yards 'guarded by a rampart of bunkers some fifty yards in front', while the eleventh required an uphill drive 'over heavy ground, bounded by rough grass and any serious deviation from the correct line will be visited by severe penalties'. The eleventh green was the one used for our present fourth hole but approached from the opposite direction.

The twelfth hole rose from the tee to a sharply sloping green and thirteen was a bogey three played back down the hill, 'a relief after the last two holes'. The fourteenth was a bogey four played to the location of the present fifth green, and would appear to have been a shorter version of the present hole. The next two holes were the present sixth and seventh, both featuring ponds, the latter requiring a 'cleverly-judged' approach to the sunken, undulating green. The seventeenth was shorter than the present eighth at 210 yards but already made use of the slope which makes the present hole so interesting. The golfers then crossed Crutch Lane for only the second time to play the final hole which is now the ninth, but which had a winter green on the site of the modern first tee. No doubt the flooding which can still affect the present ninth green necessitated a winter green on slightly higher ground.

The 1935 handbook shows that the fourth and fifth holes had been lengthened slightly, as had the twelfth, by some 85 yards and had also been 'intelligently bunkered'. Holes thirteen to seventeen were also lengthened, so the homeward nine now measured 3140 yards instead of 2900. In some cases this had been achieved by pushing the tees back but examination of the plans suggests that more accurate measuring techniques may have been employed!

When Ben Croydon was the professional he designed the new holes in 1938 which are now the seventeenth and eighteenth. Originally they were

This scene taken from the 1935 club handbook shows the fifth green in the foreground and golfers with their caddies playing to the elevated sixth green. Note the much larger copse of trees on top of the hill. Planted by John Corbett more than 100 years ago, they are a landmark for many miles. In 1996 however, only 87 of the original corsican pines remain plus a further 16 by the sixteenth green

From the 1935 club handbook. In the foreground is the winter green and bunker used when the 18th green (now the 9th) was too wet

the fifteenth and sixteenth and replaced the old ninth, tenth and eleventh for the club had lost the use of the land on which those old holes lay. Thus the last traces of Cawsey's work vanished and Braid's use of it was modified. It also created another problem for the first green had to be played twice, the second time as the seventeenth, from a different tee to the left of the first tee. This remained the case until Hawtree and Co laid out our two nines in the 1970's when more land became available after the death of Hugh Sumner. The purchase of the land occupied by the tenth hole followed in 1982. Hawtree produced two plans, the second of which was adopted and corresponds generally to the present course. However the first route following the plan only involved crossing Crutch Lane twice, the second and third holes being the present ninth and tenth, which meant that the ninth hole was across the lane. By altering the routing again, Hawtree enabled both halves of the course to finish at the clubhouse.

By re-modelling and re-routing some of Braid's holes, creating new ones such as the twelfth and making us cross the road four times instead of twice, Hawtree made good use of those natural features first observed in 1896 and later utilised by Braid. Thus two of the most celebrated architects of the century have been employed in the creation of Droitwich golf course.

We must now bring the story up to date. Mainly from the 1970's onwards each Greens Committee has made progress with the strategic planting of trees on the course. However, this did not really represent a dramatic development in policy, for way back in 1938 there is a report of 'trees planted between the third & sixteenth fairways, third & fourth, sixth & fourteenth and eighth & twelfth'. [115] It is of interest that the concern of members about trees on the course is sometimes in inverse proportion to the scale of the project. In 1985 a protest was recorded in the ladies minutes about the removal of a hawthorn tree that stood in the middle of the seventeenth fairway. But apparently without arousing comment we spent over £4,000 in 1979 (partly capital, partly grant money) on new trees and in 1995 the Forestry Commission planted at our bidding 600 trees on Green Hill. This latter project was the culmination of the Land Fill scheme originated by the Club in 1986 on a site adjacent to the twelfth fairway.

But returning to those parts of the course with which we are more familiar many members will remember that those driving off the sixth tee used to wait while those following putted out on the fifth green. Therefore the fifth green in 1988 was re-sited and made two-tier to alleviate this bottle-neck. The fifth tee was also pushed back so that the length of the hole was not significantly altered. On the seventh and eighth holes new bunkers have been created on the left side of the fairways to encourage players to drive away from the road adjacent to these holes while those within normal driving range on the right have been removed. At Chris Thompson's suggestion a long bunker now runs along the right hand side of the ninth fairway. The sand trap at the rear of the first green has been removed on the basis that the hedge is a fair hazard for the overshoot and it is hard enough to chip back onto a green which slopes away sharply. Before the 1970's there were no bunkers in front of the first but how boring to see the thinned shot roll up onto this opening green and give a false impression of an easy course.

In 1994 'Derek's Dyke' (Derek Fellows was captain at the time) was built across the tenth Fairway and first used during the playing of the Seniors' Jack Scott Cup, [116] which was appropriate as it had originally been the seniors who had called attention to the need to improve drainage on this hole although they had suggested the creation of a pond in front of the tee.

More recent developments have been the enlargement of the pond behind the ninth green, with its fountain, and the enhancement of the eighteenth tee, which, coupled with the reshaping of the bank of the Salwarpe, has created as awe-inspiring a finish as will be found anywhere.

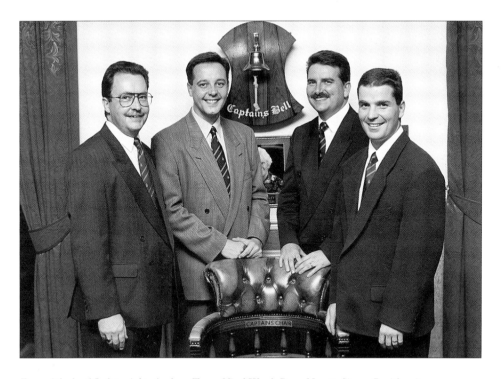

Four of the best! Left to right: Andrew Terry, Nigel Wood, Dave Nevett, Simon Braithwaite

79

CHAPTER NINE

The Professionals since 1950

SINCE WORLD War II the club had been served by five professionals and significantly more assistants. Jack Croydon had died in 1950 and was followed by Len Whiting. It would be more accurate to say that the Croydon Family were followed by the Whiting Family, for Len brought his father, Bill, with him.

Bill Whiting had a long and successful career as a professional. He won the Worcestershire Professional Foursomes in 1909 and 1910. He was club professional at Edgbaston from 1900 until 1909, moving to Walmley, where he stayed for eighteen years, and then to The Worcestershire from 1927 - 1939. His assistance and advice in the professional's shop at Droitwich were much appreciated. Bill and six out of seven brothers were professionals and in the next generation Len, his brother and three cousins were also. There used to be seven Whitings and seven Lewises playing at the Malvern Working Men's Club. 'Pop' Lewis (Cocks Moors Woods) was like an uncle to Len, who began his career with a proper uncle at Folkestone Golf Club in 1927. From there he moved to Ledbury and then to Upton-on-Severn, where he remained until the outbreak of the war.

During the war Len served as a corporal in the Pioneer Corps and took part in the D-Day Landings. After the war he went to Petersfield Golf Club in Hampshire before moving to Droitwich in 1950. His widow Betty spoke of the immense cleaning operation required in the clubhouse when they arrived. Len's mother, who was deaf and blind, and his sister, Doris, who played golf well and helped in the kitchen, also lived in the clubhouse. The Whitings were paid £5 per week out of which Betty had to pay the wages of a cleaner as well! Bill not only helped in the shop but also served behind the bar. Betty said 'We loved Droitwich' and it seems that it was not a lack of money that drove them to Oswestry Golf Club in 1953, but insecurity as the lease from Hugh Sumner was only renewed for twelve months at a time.

The supply, storage and availability of beer at Westford House will be of real concern to some readers of this book. The following anecdote illustrates what it was once necessary to do to maintain a service, which like other services, members tend to take for granted. Alterations to Westford House had meant that the normal route for the delivery of beer barrels through the east wing was no longer accessible. Betty was determined that the barrels should not be trundled through the front door and members' area. Betty appealed directly to Hugh Sumner, the club's president, and by-passed the normal channel of communication (necessary even to purchase a new broom!) - the chairman of the house committee and Hands and Evans in the company office. Hugh Sumner responded at once, visited Betty, got on the telephone to the builders and ordered the construction of a kitchen door into the front car park. Little wonder that Betty feels it should be called 'The Betty Whiting Door'!

After Oswestry Len moved to Charnwood Forest, where he was professional from 1958-76 and was made an honorary life member when he retired. He died in 1994. The affectionate feelings between the Whitings and Droitwich Golf Club were mutual. As one of our members put it: 'The Whitings were very nice people... Len was remarkable in that he didn't look like any golf pro you have ever seen... the old man was the character, had been a top notcher... he used to play with Pop Lewis and all the others round here.' [117] Francis Bird [118] further recalls 'Bill Whiting was short and always wore plus-fours'.

After Len Whiting left the club advertised the job in *Golf Illustrated* and John Freeman was appointed. He was born in 1931 in Sutton Coldfield and stayed from 1954 until 1962. John remembers the interviewing committee - the leading stalwarts of the 'struggling years' - A.V.Brackston, John Waters, the captain, a gentleman and a good friend to John Freeman, Geoff Bill, whose skilful and lively companionship on the course John was later to enjoy and remember, Bill Morgan, the lady captain and her husband Les and Mr. Roberts. John describes Brackie as the lynch pin of the club who, because of his shift work at the BBC, was able to do quite a bit of work on the course.

John attended Pitmaston Elementary School in Hall Green, leaving at fourteen to go straight into the professional's shop at the nearby Robin Hood Golf Club, where he trained with his brother under George Maisey. His daily chores included the cleaning of 250 pairs of shoes and the cleaning and maintenance of 300 sets of clubs. He had half-an-hour a day for practice. Apart from his National Service from July 1949 to July 1951, he worked with George Maisey from May 1945 until March 1954 when he came to Droitwich.

The club really needed a caterer as well but John was single. He offered to combine his professional duties with greenkeeping and so got the job. He was paid £5 a week for working five mornings a week on the course and afternoons in the professional's shop. In practice, in the summer this meant

Droitwich Professionals

Ben Croydon 1937-44

Len Whiting 1950-53

John Freeman 1954-62

Hamish Macdonald 1962-76

he mostly taught from 1.30 to 9.00 p.m. John was to have had digs with the Brackstons in their clubhouse flat, but Mrs Brackston died a few weeks before his arrival so he lived in the clubhouse with the caterers Jim and Nancy Ricketts who were like second parents to him. John mucked in, or more accurately, mucked out as he used to clean the toilets and locker rooms. He played golf at the weekends. In 1956 John came third in the Worcestershire P.G.A. Championship at Kings Norton. For recreation he joined a ballroom dancing school in Birmingham. He became engaged to a Droitwich girl in 1957 and they married two years later. The wedding reception was held in the clubhouse. He remembers his eight years at Droitwich as being very happy, 'It was fun, hard work, but fun'.

John Freeman feels the standard of golf at Droitwich improved a lot while he was there. Things seemed to take off in about 1957-58, Droitwich saw themselves less as the underdogs. There was also a large rise in membership, with whom John was very popular. In spite of this he was well aware of the financial difficulties, particularly in 1954-55 when Hugh Sumner was handing over the responsibility for the finances to the club members. Brackie had once said to him that they needed to make £45 a week from the bar to keep going.

A brief resumé of his career since he left Droitwich in May 1962 includes eighteen months as a professional in Vienna. He returned to England in 1963 when he took up the appointment at Broadway Golf Club where he has been ever since. In 1991 he handed over the professional's job to his son, although in 1996 he was still teaching golf, the aspect of the job he likes best and at which he is very gifted. He likes to go on trekking holidays.

The next professional was Hamish Macdonald, who was born in 1938 in Tain, Rosshire, in the North of Scotland, where he was educated at Tain Royal Academy. Hamish stayed at Droitwich from 1962 until 1976. His father had a handicap of two, as well as being a good footballer. Hamish started to play golf at the age of six while in Nairobi, Kenya, where he spent several years. Moving back to Scotland he attained a handicap of seven while still at school and was runner-up in the Northern Scotland Boys Championship. He left school at fifteen and went to St. Andrews as an apprentice club-maker with Robert Forgan and Sons. He was there for three or four years and left before his apprenticeship was completed to take an assistant's post at Frilford Heath in Berkshire, where he stayed for two and half years. He then went into the Royal Army Medical Corps for his national service. He played a lot of golf and in 1960 and 1961 won the Southern Command Championship at Aldershot. In the centenary Open Championship of 1960 at St. Andrews, Hamish qualified and played the first two rounds. When Hamish left the army, Ernest Cawsey of Blackwell, at the club's invitation, recommended him for the professional's job at Droitwich. Ernest was friendly with Russell

Daly who had known Hamish when he was working at Frilford Heath, so, in January 1962, he started at Droitwich.

Hamish Macdonald established a fine playing record while based at Droitwich. He came second in a play-off to Ron Moses (Worcester) in the 1968 Worcestershire Professional Championship, which was held at Blackwell. He achieved the same placing on three other occasions. Also in 1968 he played in the Midland Pro-Am with Roy Green and in 1969 he won the Worcestershire Open Championship, scoring 136 at Worcester, by beating former Midland Amateur champion Neville Newbitt in a thirty six hole play-off. He regained this title in 1973, with 138 at North Worcestershire.

In 1971 he joined a group of Worcestershire professionals who spent the winter on the South African tournament circuit, touring in 1971, 1972 and 1974, when he played in the South African Open. This was despite a heart attack in August 1972.

He resigned his position in 1976 and was made an honorary life member of the club. He left Droitwich to open a driving range in South Africa with Frank Garner, a South African professional. He was also attached to the Houghton Golf Club in Johannesburg, but his involvement in building the Fairland Golf Range on land leased from the Johannesburg Council meant that time for tournament play was limited. Partly because his wife, a St. Andrews girl whom he married when he was twenty-one, wanted to come back to Britain, he returned in December 1979. He was appointed professional at Blackwell where he stayed from 1980-91. While there only two months after recovering from a mild heart attack, he and his partner Ray Baldwin (11 handicap) came joint first in the Worcestershire President's end-of-season competition at North Worcestershire, with a six under par score of sixty three.

In 1991, after thirty-five years away, Hamish and his wife returned to Scotland, where he taught at evening classes for the Grampian Council. He also taught handicapped youngsters for the council but is now retired. He plays at Moray Golf Club and enters some senior professional tournaments and teaches three afternoons a week at the Spey Bay Golf Club, not 500 yards from the Spey Estuary. Hamish has belonged to St. Andrews Golf Club since he was sixteen and is now a country member. He has an ambition to take up fishing.

Hamish Macdonald made many friends and no enemies while he was at Droitwich. He would not have stayed fourteen years if he had not settled in and enjoyed it, but he does remember with some poignancy the primitiveness of the professional's shop/shed by the first tee. The wind whistled through it: it was like an ice box in winter and because it had a tin roof it could be an oven in the summer.

In May 1995 he returned to Blackwell to play in the inaugural 'Senior Club Professional Championship'. He was disappointed to score 82 and 79 and thereby miss the cut.

One of Hamish's assistants was Bob Gould and his record is worthy of inclusion.

Bob Gould was assistant professional from 1968-74. Born in 1951, his original ambition was to join the R.A.F. but his maths were not good enough. He recalls taking 145 strokes in his first round of golf but within eighteen months was down to a handicap of two, with the help of Hamish Macdonald's coaching. He made a successful application to be Mike Busk's assistant at the Mid-Ocean Club in Bermuda, for which there were an estimated 250 applicants. He never finished lower than third in a tournament there. Unfortunately his work permit ran out and he returned to live with his family in Droitwich in 1977. In November of that year he was appointed professional at Chipping Norton, where he remained until 1996. Bob then accepted the position as professional at Palmerston North, New Zealand.

Bob was co-designer of 'The Garden Driving Range', a gadget to help you learn golf in the confines of your garden, which he demonstrated on Central Television. He has happy memories of his time at Droitwich where he used to repair clubs in an old tractor shed on the site of the rear car park. He made persimmon headed clubs and still uses this type today despite the popularity of metal woods. Bob's father, Gordon, was assistant to Ben Croydon at Droitwich from 1937 to 1939.

Chris Thompson, who was born in Harborne in 1953, followed Hamish Macdonald. It says a lot for Droitwich Golf Club that in thirty-five years we have had only two professionals. Moreover we have been undoubtedly lucky to have secured and retained the services of two such talented, hard-working and above all friendly professionals. Chris comes from a golfing family. His father was professional at Harborne Church Farm, moving to Marston Green in 1958. He went to Hatchford Brook in 1969 when that course opened and retired in 1985 after a lifetime working at municipal courses in the Birmingham area. Chris' grandfather was an assistant professional and his great uncle a pro who went all over the world including the Royal Bombay Club and New Zealand. His Godfather was Jack Cawsey, for whom Chris' father worked at Pype Hayes just after the war and who was the son of George Cawsey who laid out our original course in Bays Meadow in 1896.

There is a photograph of Chris aged four or five, swinging a golf club. His first set of clubs arrived when he was eight. He caddied for his father and by the time he was sixteen had reduced his handicap from thirty six to two. After leaving Coleshill Grammar School with seven 'O' levels at the age of sixteen he worked for his father at Hatchford Brook for three months, never having considered a career in anything other than golf. When the three months were up he got a position at Copt Heath with Brian Barton, who had worked for Chris' father as an assistant. Here he played regularly with Peter McEvoy, who became British Amateur Champion in 1977 & 78 and played in the Walker Cup Team, which he subsequently captained. He and Chris spent one whole winter practising pitching, putting and bunker shots in competition with each other. During his time as an assistant he won the Warwickshire Assistants stroke play championship in 1975 and 1976, adding the Assistants Match play title in 1976, which was also the year of the first of three victories in the Davenports Par 3 Competition, held on the short course at Kings Norton.

Chris Thompson played the course for the first time in the 1976 Phoenix Metals Pro-Am, partnered by the club captain, Tony Ives. He took up his post as club professional on 1st October of that year and from then on continued an impressive catalogue of tournament successes. He won the Midland Open in 1976 and again in 1982, being interviewed on BRMB's Tony Butler show by their golf reporter Don Jones on the former occasion.

Chris Thompson drives off on his way to winning the Worcsestershire Matchplay Championship in 1984. In the final he beat Bill Firkins (Stourbridge) at the 19th
Looking on in the front row, left to right: Jim & Sylvia Gray, Chris Thompson's parents, Madeline George, Bill Ross, Gordon Cooper
Back row: Pete Lancaster, Colin Brade, Gil Taylor, Alan Nicholls, Duncan Stuart

He won the Davenports Par 3 Competition again in 1979 and 1982, demonstrating his skill with the eleven iron to such effect that he scored two holes in one in the 1982 tournament, prompting the Birmingham Post's correspondent to describe him as 'the region's undisputed short-course specialist'.

He proved he was more than that in the same year when he set a new record of 65 at the North Worcestershire course in a Pro-Am, a record that was never broken as the course was changed shortly afterwards. Since then Kevin Dickens has returned a 63 on the revised lay-out. 1984 was another good year in which Chris came third in the Midland Telford Ironmasters Tournament and won the Worcestershire Professional Match Play Championship, a feat he repeated in 1988.

Chris Thompson's work has stretched beyond the confines of his Droitwich shop, however, as he has been a major figure in the Worcestershire Professional Golfers Association. He became competitions secretary shortly after his arrival in Droitwich, captain in 1980 and then chairman of the committee. He then became secretary in the early 80's in succession to Eric Booy, the Fulford Heath professional who had done the job for thirty years. Eric died in 1994. Chris was elected President in 1987, only the fourth professional to be given that honour after Bill Firkins Snr, 'Pop' Lewis and Bernard Preston. It was with Preston that Chris started the monthly medals for the assistants in 1983. These competitions have increased from two to twenty four a year.

Chris finally resigned from the W.P.G.A, in 1992 and was made an honorary life member, an honour he greatly appreciated. Soon after this he had his first knee operation, an ongoing problem which has restricted his competitive career.

As a teacher Chris is much in demand and tells some amusing stories about his experiences. He used to take evening classes for the Sports Council and the C.C.P.R. At a Birmingham school on one occasion he told a pupil, as this was a phrase in his repertoire, to 'throw the clubhead at the target'. He had turned away and then heard a mighty crash - the pupil had taken him literally and let go of the club which penetrated the ceiling and hung there. On another occasion in a school assembly hall another pupil let go of his club, which luckily missed everybody and crashed through the windows of the headmaster's office at the end of the hall!

His teaching also includes the training of his assistants, all of whom have passed their exams and progressed well in their careers. Chris always gets on with his assistants, but was particularly sorry to lose Martin Griffin, who was more a friend than employee. He left to join another of Chris' former assistants, Mike Deeley at La Moye Golf Club in Jersey.

Mike was assistant professional from October 1976 and stayed until 1981. Born in 1959, he was introduced to golf at a very early age as his mother used to push him around Redditch golf course on her trolley! However the family influence was less strong than that of his friends and he did not start playing seriously until he joined them for games after school. He first played at Royal St. Davids, Harlech in 1972, as his father ran a sports shop in Barmouth. He was encouraged to remain at school with the result that one of his eight 'O'levels includes a pass in Welsh.

Playing off a handicap of four he won the Prince of Wales Trophy, among others, with the result that juniors were subsequently banned from the competition! When the family returned to the midlands he worked for Frank Powell at Redditch and it was Frank who pointed out the advertisement for the Droitwich job to him. Chris Thompson trained him well and he passed his P.G.A. exams as well as winning a number of tournaments. Mike once scored a hole in one at our thirteenth hole, albeit it was a winter green. While on the subject of remarkable scoring it is recorded that Keith Brooks once scored a two (an albatross) at our fifth hole.

For eighteen months from 1981 he was sponsored as a full time tournament player by a number of generous Droitwich members and then became teaching professional at Brocton Hall in Staffordshire. From there he moved to Matlock where he remained until 1993 when he landed his present prestigious appointment at La Moye in Jersey. His wife Jenny is also a fine golfer and won the Worcestershire Ladies Championship in 1991.

Chris also keeps in touch with Barry Higgins who is now a professional in Germany, while David Philp went to Denmark.

Chris Thompson is always ready with expert advice when asked for it. Many of the low handicap golfers currently playing at Droitwich originally learned the game from Chris, not least among them John Bickerton Jnr, who began as an eleven year old. He is now a full member of the P.G.A. European Tour and an honorary life member of the club. 1995 was his first full season on the tour and, having qualified through the satellite tour, he returned some capable performances to retain his card for 1996. At one stage in the Open Championship at St. Andrews in 1995 he seemed to be in a strong position until the weather changed dramatically, dashing his hopes as well as those of his many supporters at Droitwich and, indeed, in all of Worcestershire. All members benefit equally from Chris' imagination, dedication and skills. In one club competition, for example, he stood on the first tee and videoed the swings of the participating members, showing the resulting film later in the clubhouse. Quite rightly, Droitwich does not take Chris Thompson for granted, following as he does the excellent tradition of our professionals over one hundred years.

Another professional who began as a junior, first under Hamish Macdonald's tutelage and then that of Chris Thompson, was David Eddiford, the son of John, who resumed membership in 1975 after a ten year break due to illness, to facilitate his son's membership. As a youngster John had played cricket with Roy Fabricius and remembers being driven dangerously to matches by Roy's father, 'Old Fab'.

David had an impressive junior and amateur record before turning professional in 1991, when he became an assistant at Kings Norton. One of his amateur achievements was the setting of a course record at Droitwich in 1983. He also had a successful career in the county team and was county champion in 1982, 1986 and 1990.

There is no doubt though that Chris' biggest success has been the progress of John Bickerton. John caddied for his father when he was eight and couldn't wait to take the game up himself, eventually joining the club in 1980, having attended the classes organised in 1979 by Jim Gray and run by Chris Thompson. He was a regular truant from Droitwich High School but his teachers were sufficiently sympathetic to enquire about his golf when he returned to lessons.

Jim Gray was then in charge of the county boys and picked John to play for the team in 1982. He had already come to the attention of Peter Ricketts by this time, having beaten the golf journalist by three & two and by reducing his handicap from thirteen to eight in the space of two days in his school holidays. 1986 was a triumphant year for John. He became club champion and Worcestershire Junior Champion, beating Darren Prosser at Malvern by one shot in scoring 143. He also helped the Droitwich boys win the Mirams Salver for the team event for the third successive year. The year was crowned, however, by his participation in the first English Boys County Championship. Worcestershire qualified for the final by winning the Midlands qualifying event at Sleaford, although John did not play in this event.

The finals were at Sandy Lodge where Worcestershire played Sussex, Durham and Gloucestershire in a Round Robin. The first match was halved against Gloucestershire. On the second day Worcestershire beat Sussex 6-3 and destroyed Durham by 8-1 on the last day. It is worth recording the event in such detail because of the massive contribution made by Droitwich, through John and Jim Gray and it is also of monumental importance to the County Union.

It was participation in this glorious victory that brought John Bickerton to the attention of the English selectors the following year. He played for England Boys against Scotland and Ireland in the boys home internationals and thereby became Droitwich's first international representative. He played for the county's first team and also won the Ludlow Scratch Open.

In 1988 he won the Boulton Salver partnered by Simon Braithwaite, the Worcestershire Amateur Matchplay, the Worcestershire Amateur Championship Silver Medal, the inaugural Kings Norton Scratch Open for the Oak Trophy, the Birmingham Post and Mail Champion of Champions and kept his place in the England boys team. In addition he was in the Droitwich team which won the Brand Hall Gold Vase.

1989 saw even more progress for John Bickerton attained a plus handicap. He played for England youths against Scotland, won the French Nations Cup with Gary Evans at Bondues G.C. near Paris and the Nick Faldo Commemoration Jug at Welwyn Garden City setting a new course record of 65 in the first round. He partnered Joe Higgins of Patshull Park in the Ping-Pro-Scratch Tournament at Gains-borough and won it. He finished second in the West of England Championship at Taunton and in the Worcestershire championship, which was won by club-mate Simon Braithwaite. John remembers his umbrella being struck by lightning on this occasion and vividly recalls the spark travelling down the umbrella and along his arm.

John Bickerton receives the Nick Faldo commemoration jug from the man himself, 1989

He also won the County Amateur Championship, retained his Champion of Champions title and won the Ashton Vase. In fifty-one tournaments he played in 1989 and 1990 he finished in the top five seventeen times and twenty-seven times in the top ten, improving his amateur ranking from thirty second to eleventh and reducing his handicap to + 2.2.

Nick Faldo invited him back to Welwyn Garden City for his Master Class where John joined twenty-five other amateurs and young professionals. Here he saw a very different Nick Faldo from the normal press portrait of the champion golfer. John received coaching from David Leadbetter, Dennis Sheehy, Mitchell Spearman, Dennis Pugh and Paul Ankers. He was also invited to Spain for England team coaching where the coach, John Stirling, talked in his report of John's 'uninhibited abandon' in play and his 'lovely manner'.

1990 continued well for John. He played in the British Amateur at Muirfield, beating English international John Metcalfe in the first round. He went on to win the Midland Amateur Open at Little Aston and Sutton Coldfield in June. It is said lightning never strikes twice, but this time it was John's putter which was struck as he faced a holeable putt, which he duly made, having preferred to putt rather than take shelter. He won the tournament by eight shots, finishing nine under par.

The 1990 Worcestershire Matchplay Championship was held at Droitwich and not surprisingly the club was well represented, John beating Simon Braithwaite in the semi-final and David Eddiford in an exciting final. In this tournament John played 61 holes in 19 under par. He won the Worcestershire Open Championship and represented England Youths again. It was not until 1991 that John Bickerton had his first hole in one, which he achieved on the eighteenth at Droitwich in a friendly four ball. He went on to win the Berkshire Trophy and the County Championship, using a driver and two wood borrowed from Terry Shingler, who was an England selector, as he had broken his driver at The Berkshire. After coming second in the Tillman Trophy John turned professional.

On 6th June 1992 he qualified for the next stage of the Open Championship in the area qualifier at Blackwell. In 1994 he played on the European Challenge tour and recorded his first tour win in the Gore-tex Open when he defeated Lee Vannett in a sudden death play-off after they had tied on 280, twelve under par. His success on the Challenge tour earned him his card for the main European tour. The club marked this by presenting him with a plaque detailing his scores on the challenge tour. Later a shot-gun competition was arranged in his honour, in which John partnered every group by playing the eighteenth with them, his score counting towards their Stableford totals.

On 17th-18th March 1995 John Bickerton Jnr, aged twenty-five and playing only his eleventh tour event wrote his name in the European tour record books at the Portuguese Open at Penha Longa, near Estoril. His second round on Friday was interrupted by bad weather after he had scored four consecutive birdies. When he restarted the round on Saturday he scored another four birdies, missing a sixty foot putt, which would have made it nine consecutive birdies, on the sixteenth. This equalled the tour record set by Severiano Ballesteros in 1985 and subsequently matched by Ian Woosnam and Tony Johnstone. Par for the course was 72 and John's scores were 72, 68 and 74. His feat was described as 'an amazing burst'.

In April 1995 John partnered Darren Lee in the Perrier Pairs event at St. Cloud. It was a better ball competition and they led after the first round with a score of 59 but eventually finished seventeenth equal. In the Open at St. Andrews John had a fine first round of 71, one under par, but sadly faltered to an 80 in the second round when the strong winds affected play late in the afternoon.

John Bickerton was elected an honorary life member of Droitwich Golf Club at the 1995 A.G.M., an honour given for special services to the club or in special circumstances. Seconding the proposal made by the captain Derek Fellows, Geoff Hudspith said he was 'unassuming, natural and had his feet on the ground'. He was 'something special'. On the 1995 tour John played in twenty eight tournaments, making the cut in seventeen of them. He won £48,000 against £32,000 in expenses. His caddy is sixty-two year old Scottie Gilmore who caddied for Tony Jacklin when Tony was at his best. He has also caddied for Lanny Wadkins, Greg Norman (for three years) and Lee Trevino.

John's 1996 tour got off to an unfortunate start. In February he went to Sun City in South Africa and was one under par after the first round when he was disqualified for marking his own card, after an official had mistakenly handed cards to the players themselves rather than their markers. It was the first time he has ever been disqualified and there were extenuating circumstances.

Chris Thompson is still John's mentor and no one understands his natural swing better than Chris. John values the role that physical fitness plays in developing mental fitness and still includes running in his winter training programme, covering about five miles in a session. John, who is most generous in his tributes to all whom he meets, very much appreciates the financial and mental help that Droitwich Golf Club has given him and still does give him. He is sure that we have a special spirit here.

The Morris family, of whom the senior member, Ted, is a Droitwich member, have developed the Bromsgrove Golf Centre and also support John by giving him free use of the driving range.

Three more recent juniors who have benefited sufficiently from Chris Thompson's tuition to merit selection for the county boys team have been Lee Priddey, Lee Jones and Gavin Bourne, whose father, Terry was captain in 1995. The first of this trio had an especially good season in 1995, winning the Bill Cunningham Trophy for the most successful player in the team.

CHAPTER TEN

Droitwich Welcomes All Sportsmen

I T HAS already been established how the interests of the hotels, brine baths and the golf course overlapped in the development of Droitwich Spa. Even if those coming for treatment were unable or unwilling to play, these patients were supported by family or friends for whom recreation was a necessity. Indeed in the words of the club captain in 1903, [119] quoted in the Droitwich Guardian: 'The club originated in a desire to provide for the better class of visitors a means of recreation. It was to be an attraction to induce such people to come here and to prolong their stay when here'.

Many advertisements point out the proximity of the hotels and the golf course. The Whitehall Review of 18th April 1908 praised the Royal Hotel as having:

'Facilities for tennis, golf and croquet... Queen Victoria stayed there when a girl of thirteen'. The article goes on to recommend 'the healthiness of the environment... a good place for recreation and rest... the district itself is too well known to need description. Nothing in our opinion could excel it for healthiness and abundance of pure air, water and sunshine. The district must necessarily possess special interest to clubmen, sportsmen... Mrs. Dunn is unremitting in her attention to the care and comfort of guests. The key-note of the establishment is comfort and there is a home-like atmosphere very pleasing to the visitor from afar.... There is every possible recreation available within a short radius. Anyone who wishes to enjoy a really restful holiday will find no finer spot than here. Cuisine, service, prices, wine cellar are of a high standard for outside London. The whole neighbourhood is singularly rich both in natural beauty and the most delightful historical association. All these advantages have greatly helped to make Droitwich the most efficacious sanatorium in the world. No more comfortable hotel can be found in the kingdom. The visitor received that close and personal attention to his needs to be found in so few hotels.'

Over a quarter of a century later the link between the hotels and golf is still present as we can see in the 1935 Droitwich Spa Handbook, in which both the Raven and Park hotels advertise themselves as having a nine hole putting course. It was not unknown for Droitwich hotels to arrange putting competitions against each other and this was even quoted in the London

The putting green at the Worcestershire Brine Baths in 1905

Press 'golf putting matches and tennis matches were often held on hotel lawns'. [120] In 1939 Droitwich Golf Club in a big advertisement is highlighted with Norbury House, St. Andrews Brine Baths and the Winter Gardens. It is described as having one of the best courses in the Midlands. In an article called 'Football and Golf', written in 1903, [121] the author, William McGregor, quoted Dr. Robinson, himself a footballer and golfer, who claimed that the footballer got physical benefits from golf. 'I am strongly of the opinion that it would greatly strengthen the knee-joints and chiefly develop the muscles of the loin, back and chest as well as of the arms'. Elsewhere in the article McGregor says that the professional footballer 'has a great deal of spare time on his hands'. What is certain is that for whatever reasons, whether for recreation or for mental and physical benefit professional footballers have often and do often play golf. Michael Parkinson, assigned to interview ex-footballer Gary Lineker chose to conduct the interview on the golf course. The article in *The Daily Telegraph* of 22nd April 1995, has a heading that will strike a chord with all golfers: 'The squeaky clean face of football lets his halo slip on the golf course; the moment Lineker lost his claim to sainthood'.

Football teams come to Droitwich because the hotels are good and are convenient for many of the footballing venues in the Midlands; they come so that their players can be treated in the brine baths and to relax on the golf course. As every football fan will tell you it is more a question of which teams have not stayed in Droitwich than those which have.

For example, Nottingham Forest came to Droitwich in 1952 at the bidding of their manager Billy Walker who, 'as a former Aston Villa player, knows Droitwich so very well. Not only did Billy Walker come in the past for brine 'pep' treatment, but also for a round of golf on the pleasant local course'. [122] Wolverhampton Wanderers and England captain Billy Wright played our course and had to return for his golf shoes.

Another international who played was Danny Blanchflower, who led Northern Ireland to the World Cup quarter-finals in 1958. He played for Aston Villa from 1951-4 and in 1953, partnering an Aston Villa colleague, Tommy Thompson, he won the Corbett Bowl. Tommy Thompson partnering our own Dave Walsh was joint third in the same competition in 1955. In 1965 Sunderland F.C. stayed at the Chateau Impney Hotel in preparation for their match with West Bromwich Albion. The Bromsgrove Messenger reported that the Sunderland players Dominic Sharkey, Cecil Irwin, John Parke and Billy Campbell played eighteen holes on our course.

Some visiting footballers have been so charmed with our course that they have stayed on as members, prominent among them being Dave Walsh,

Plenty of room for a slice at the 4th hole in the 1960's. It is now the 15th

who was born in Waterford and played for Ireland. In 1946 he transferred from Linfield to West Bromwich Albion whose players were associate members of Droitwich Golf Club. Dave Walsh became a full member when he moved to Aston Villa in 1950 having scored over 100 goals for West Bromwich. Dave became captain of Droitwich Golf Club in 1966 and president in 1979-80. He served on committees for twenty one years. He married and settled in Droitwich where he had a sports outfitters. Best man at his wedding was another Irish international, Jack Vernon, who captained West Bromwich Albion and also was a member of Droitwich. Dave retired to Thurlestone in South Devon, where he still enjoys playing golf. He is an honorary life member of Droitwich Golf Club.

Dave Walsh and Ron Wall, who had a butcher's shop in Droitwich, had a regular four-ball with two local boys, Jim Bourne and Jimmy Duggan. They used to play for the meal. Jim Bourne, born in Droitwich in 1914, was a porter at the Worcestershire Hotel for twenty six years. He also worked at the Norbury Hotel and the Giffard Hotel in Worcester. While he was Head Porter at the Worcestershire he brought Chesney Allen, the famous comedian, to play snooker at the golf club with himself, Geoff Bill, Brackie and Colin Brade. Jim is over six foot one and known for his good looks. He was a Military Policeman during the war and was taken prisoner in Java. At his camp 1,500 men died in three and a half years and only 308 survived. He played off ten and won a Phoenix Pro-am partnering Bernard Preston of Rose Hill Golf Club. He also won the Eric Griffin in 1967 and the Shirley Jones in 1977. He played all over the place, using the book of county tickets which entitled members to play all the courses in Worcestershire on weekdays. He played in some competitions with Chris Thompson.

Jim's daughter, Sylvia, when sixteen and playing off twenty four, won the Harry Whitehouse playing with Ron Wall.

Jim Bourne's partner was Jimmy Duggan, whose brother Cyril used to caddy at the club and described Jimmy with much affection as the 'joker in the pack'. Jimmy was born in 1920 and died of cancer in May 1982. He expressly did not wish to be mourned as he had a good life. He used to enter a float at the Droitwich Carnival every year and loved gambling on the dogs and the horses, his greengrocers shop being conveniently close to the bookmakers in Droitwich.

He was always chatting to visitors and passers-by and ready at any time for a game of golf. Jimmy's grandfather and two of his uncles played professional football. In 1936 Jimmy was apprenticed to West Ham, then moved with his Uncle Tommy to West Bromwich Albion for whom he played as an inside forward until the war.

In the war Jimmy served as a signaller in the Royal Navy. There was a picture of him in the *Droitwich Guardian* of 3rd March 1945 'receiving a trophy as captain of the champion team in a Navy Football League in the Middle East.... While at Tripoli he was selected for Ireland v. England Services International Match.' He possibly owed his selection to the fact that his grandfather was Irish. After the war Jimmy went off to Australia for twelve months or so and was player/manager of Swan Athletic. In 1952, towards the end of his playing career he was appointed player/manager of Bromsgrove Rovers. His second wife Pat and their two daughters have survived him.

Jimmy's politics, which were little discussed, were conservative. His attitude was that 'if you are prepared to work for it, you're entitled to benefit from it'. He could deflate pretentious people. 'If he was with upper class people he would make sure he was just himself, with no airs or graces or what-have-you'. He built his greengrocers shop himself, although DIY was not his strong suit. In 1961, playing off four with Pauline Cook off thirty six, he won the Ludlow mixed foursomes. Pauline was a fifteen year old schoolgirl who had played since she was twelve, using just four cut-down clubs. Her father caddied for her.

Among Jimmy's other victories were the Brand Hall Gold Vase, at Kings Norton in 1961, with Roy Green, Dave Walsh and Percy Harris. Their score was 288. This trophy was won again by Droitwich in 1988 and 1996. On the latter occasion Simon Braithwaite broke the Kidderminster course record with a 65. In 1963 Jimmy won both the Kingsman Cup, with Dave Walsh as his partner, and the Boulton Salver, with Roy Green, at Worcester with a score of 141.

Jimmy had taken to golf like a duck to water and likewise in the seventies he had instant success when he took up bowls. He represented the county within a year and played regularly in the National Championships at Worthing. Jimmy was a larger than life character, whose epitaph might be that he always had a smile on his face.

The only other professional footballer who is currently a member is Kenny Barrett of Aston Villa, but this is not the last connection with football. Mike Taylor, who followed Ray Baldwin as secretary in 1987, had previously played before becoming a referee.

The brief mention of snooker is the cue to mention snooker at Droitwich Golf Club. The Droitwich and District Snooker League was founded in 1963 and the golf club were the first champions. We have won many team and individual honours since then and were particularly successful in the 70's and early 80's with present members Sid Turton, Bob Burnett, Colin Brade and Barry Joule prominent. During those years and until the mid 80's the club ran three or four teams.

97

Now only one team plays, with Barry Joule the only survivor from the 'glory days'. Brian Bishop who played for the snooker A team has supplied this information. He is well remembered by his contemporaries at Kings Norton Grammar School as a hard-hitting, window smashing batsman and is caricatured in a Norman Edwards cartoon of Bournville Athletic Club's nineteenth annual inter-departmental sports with the caption 'What an all-rounder! Cricket, tennis, hockey, soccer, badminton and shove-'apenny!' How Norman Edwards found all this out we do not know, but suspect Brian Bishop told him! Brian was captain of the club in 1989. Before closing this brief interlude on snooker it is right to record that one of our tables was presented by T. Harold Platts [123] and his son Derek. The table had previously been at the Clarendon Hotel. It was also Harold Platts who in 1936, presented the Raven Bowl.

It is not only football and professional footballers who have a link with golf. The tie-up between cricket, professional cricketers and golf is also very secure. Very many of our members are ex-cricketers and always have been since the beginnings of the club. Some cricket clubs folded up in the early years of this century because their members had transferred their allegiance to golf.

In 1991 our most illustrious member, Graeme Hick of Worcestershire C.C.C. and England invited Ian Botham to play in our invitation day. Ian Rone, who has also been on Worcestershire's books, won the day with his partner, but Ian Botham is also remembered for driving the twelfth, ignoring

An aerial view of the course, c. 1979

1975 AGM group. Left to right, Back row: Olive Young, Mary Waters, Doris Brittain, Margaret Groom, Dorothy Hill, Dorothy Griffin, Bill Morgan. Front row: Gwyneth Presley-Jones, Joyce Haigh, Billie Lippett, Margaret Shaw

Worcestershire County Officers 1992 & 1993. Left to right: Sylvia Gray (treasurer), Marion Lancaster (secretary), Betty Pryce-Jones (president), Ros Weston (captain), Jenny Harrison (competition secretary)

County Handicap League Champions 1993. Droitwich won again in 1994. The team from left to right: Helen Cocks, Muriel Somerville, Chris Mayneord, Linda Ottway, Sylvia Gray

Lady Past Captain's Day 1996
Left to right. Standing: M. Somerville, M. Talbot, O.Young, C. Mayneord, L. Ottway, I. Taylor, A. Price, R. Weston, J, Harvey, N. Williams, J. Phillips, P. Tattersall, J. Harrison
Seated: M. Shaw, M. Groom, S. Gray, P. Bradley, K. Bill, M. Lancaster

The ladies section 1996. In the front row 3rd from left is centenary captain, Sylvia Gray. On her left is 1996 captain Pat Bradley, next to whom is the president, Marion Lancaster

Past Captains Day 1975. Left to right: Barry Joule, Ron Wall, Norman Baker, Dave Walsh, Gilly Gilmore, Les Morgan, Harvey Hill, Tony Ives, John Waters, Frank Ashenden, Geoff Bill, Bill Best, Ivan Bedford, A.V. Brackston, Percy Rishworth

Worcestershire led by Jim Gray of Droitwich (front row on right). Winners of the English Boys County Championship 1986. John Bickerton (2nd from left in back row) was a member of this team

January 1995. Is it a flood or a new water hazard?

The 12th green

DROITWICH GOLF AND COUNTRY CLUB 1897

Past captains day 1994. Left to right, Back row: Rod Mayneord, Geoff Hudspith, Brian Bishop, Bob Carter, John Mole, Bryn Harrington, Colin Brade. Middle row: Gilly Gilmore, Jim Gray, Tony Cox, Bob Tunstall, Warren Davies, Barry Joule, Peter Pessol, Ray Woodhead, Barry Tomkins, Albert Lippett, Charles Harrison, Ivan Bedford. Front row: Harold Cartwright, Norman Baker, Geoff Bill, Derek Fellows, Les Morgan, Dave Walsh, Ron Wall

Centenary, development and general committee members September 1996. Left to right, Back row: Duncan Stuart, John Bromhead, David Pulling, John Weston, Clive Marsh. Middle row: Peter Pessol, Chris Gupwell, Peter Brannon, Mike Nolan, Mal Hughes, Geoff Potter, Sylvia Gray, Derek Fellows. Front row: Pat Bradley, Geoff Hudspith, Ian Rone, Walter Jarvis, Terry Bourne

The clubhouse with new extension, September 1996

the dog-leg. Graeme also introduced the present England captain, Mike Atherton and Neil Fairbrother of Lancashire C.C.C. and England.

We do not have the complete picture of professional cricketers who have played at or visited our club but what we have is interesting. The visitors' book for September 1993 records the signatures of the following Lancashire players, who came after their match against Worcestershire: Mike Atherton, Nick Speak, Gary Yates, John Crawley, Mike Watkinson , Philip de Freitas (the last three all England players) and Warren Hegg. You can also spot three internationals among the Middlesex C.C.C. visitors who came a fortnight later: Richard Johnson, Mark Feltham, Mark Ramprakash, Angus Fraser, Philip Tufnell and physiotherapist Simon Sheppard. Finally, no less a person than Geoffrey Boycott used our putting green in 1991.

We have referred to John Bickerton Jnr's running as part of his training for golf, but one of our members, Bill Hawkley, was a runner par excellence. Bill ran the 800m and 1500m and was Bromsgrove Athletic Club's first international representative. He competed against France in Paris and in the home internationals against Northern Ireland, Scotland and Wales between 1945-1947.

Let us now turn our attention to the professional golfers who have played on our course. George Cawsey, who designed our original lay out, has already been described. He returned to Droitwich in 1909 to play in a four-ball match in which he partnered the Rev. F.D. Richardson and defeated Lindsay Ross, the club professional, and A.C. Pickering.

In the late 1920's the Birmingham City footballer, Jack Russell and his partner Arthur Skett, a four handicapper, used to play two professionals at Droitwich off scratch. Russell was born in 1904 and was a professional footballer for twenty years. He had a trial for Worcestershire C.C.C. as a fast left arm bowler. Having started as a caddy at the North Worcestershire Club, he played off scratch. His grandson, David Russell (Kedleston Park) has been on the P.G.A. European Tour for over twenty years and his great grandson, aged twelve is playing off nine.

Jack was not supposed to play golf during the week after Thursday, but used to play a round at Rose Hill on Saturday mornings before going on to St. Andrews in the afternoon. He remembers seeing horses pulling a gang-mower but our course was in very poor condition when he played it: 'It was like a ploughed field, the greens were awful but the beer was good'. [124]

The professionals Jack and Arthur played against were Jess Partridge, who was born in 1893 and was professional at Rose Hill for many years and Bill Adwick of Walsall Golf Club. Jess Partridge came from Chipping Norton and was assistant to George Buckle when George was at North Worcestershire. Bill Adwick was a tall ex-grenadier guardsman, who had a plate in his head from a war injury. Before going to Walsall he had been at Copt Heath and Harborne Municipal.

The next professional reported to have played at Droitwich and who became one of the best known and most popular Midlands professionals, was 'Pop' Lewis, called 'Pop' because of his short temper, although to meet him casually you would not realise this. He is the undisputed father-figure of the Midlands golf world. He was born on 25th April 1908 one of seven brothers who were all members of the Malvern Working Men's Club, as noted above. He was assistant professional at North Worcestershire and Kings Norton before going into partnership with his father at Cocks Moors Woods, where he served from 1945 until 1970. He was still active as starter for Worcestershire Golf Union Membership Scheme meetings until a few years ago.

Following Pop as assistant to Ernest Cawsey at Kings Norton was Bernard Preston. He described Cawsey as 'a wonderful man, very fair and one of the few really good men I have met'. At Droitwich Bernard won the Phoenix Metals Pro-Am partnering Jimmy Duggan. He was professional at Kings Norton from 1945-1959 when he moved to Rose Hill where he stayed until 1979. He played in the Open Championship every year for twenty years.

The most internationally well-known golfer to have played our course is undoubtedly Ian Woosnam, who played in our Pro-Am on 28th August 1979. He was born in Oswestry in 1958 and turned professional in 1976. He was third in the Open in 1986 and runner-up in the U.S. Open in 1989, but his greatest triumph was the Masters at Augusta in 1991. His best year though was 1987 when he won a number of events including the Suntory World Match Play and the Individual title in the World Cup, when he represented Wales with David Llewellyn. He has played in every Ryder Cup since 1983, although he was only called into the victorious 1995 team as a late replacement for Jose Maria Olazabal.

Another Ryder Cup player played in the same Pro-Am as Ian Woosnam, the Notts professional from Hollinwell, Brian Waites. He was born in 1940 and turned professional in 1957. He performed mainly in Midland events until a successful season on the European tour brought him to a wider public and continued success led to a Ryder Cup place. More recently he was lucky to escape with his life in a horrendous car accident, from which he has made a courageous recovery enabling him to compete once again, but on the Senior tour. He has also represented England in the World Cup, in 1980, 1982 and 1983.

The competition which attracted these professionals was begun on the initiative of Bill Ross, whose company was Phoenix Metals. Bill joined the club in 1948 and remained a member until his death in September 1996,

100

except during the Suez Crisis, when petrol rationing was threatened. He was a vice-president of the Worcestershire P.G.A. In planning the tournament he took advice from the president of the P.G.A. Dennis Shirlaw of Kidderminster, our professional, Hamish Macdonald and Peter Ricketts the golf journalist and a member of Kidderminster Golf Club.

The first record we have is of the 1970 Tournament. It was advertised as 'The Phoenix Metals £300 Professional Golf Tournament' and was a thirty-six holes stroke play championship played on Thursday, 4th June. Twenty-six professionals competed. Then it became a two day weekend event, still for professionals, but this proved to be unpopular with the Droitwich members, so the competition, which ran for eleven years, became the Phoenix Metals Pro-am. Between twenty and thirty four-balls would compete, with three fee-paying amateurs in each group. Phoenix Metals provided prize money to add to the entry fees but when the P.G.A. demanded higher levels of prize-money than deemed practical, the tournament was discontinued. Bill Ross was also a keen chess player, who played regularly for the county and won the Worcestershire County Championship in the late fifties. Bill continued to enjoy his golf, using a four wheel buggy mainly at Ombersley, until shortly before his death.

In the 1971 Pro-Am John Lower of Burton-on-Trent broke the professional record with 64. Two years later in the same event Richard Livingston reduced this to 61. He was partnered by Colin Brade (Captain 1992) who clearly remembers the achievement:

'9 pars and 9 birdies; he never missed a green. It was steady, copybook golf. His score could have been under sixty as he had several puttable putts that did not drop. For two or three years at that time he was the best pro in the midlands.'

Colin Brade also had a marvellous round. He was playing off five and only dropped three shots. In spite of this he only came in on one hole – 'it was frustrating really'. Richard Livingston later became the professional at South Herts which was Dai Rees' old club. At the time of this Pro-Am he was professional at Ladbrook Park, at which club Bill Ross was also a member.

Phoenix Metals furnished the dining room, gave the board room table and the flag pole as well as contributing steps and other furniture on the course.

When the event became, simply, The Droitwich Pro-am in 1979 David Dunk set a new course record for the revised course. His sixty four, which according to the Birmingham Evening Mail 'featured a homeward half of thirty in which Dunk only had eleven putts', was four shots better than the next professional's score and his team consisting of Brian Lawrence, John

Ganner and Peter Ward won by two clear shots, a large margin in such an event.

In 1956 there was a unique and light-hearted match in which our golfers played against a team of archers. This was reported as;

Golfers challenge Archers - eighteen 'hole' match at Droitwich. Fourteen members of Droitwich Golf Club will set out tomorrow, Saturday, for an eighteen hole match with a difference for they will be competing against archers. The mixed team from the golf club will take on a team consisting of members from the Piers Plowman Archery Club, Malvern, who will hole out by hitting a white cardboard disc four inches in diameter placed flat on the ground level with the hole. 'The golf club has challenged us to a match' explained Mr. E. Ashton, secretary of Piers Plowman, 'archery golf is in an experimental stage and recently the rules were altered because they slightly favoured the archers'. [Rules follow this quotation.] [125]

The next week in the paper there were descriptions and photos of the match which the golf club won six and a half to four and a half.

Not only professional sportsmen have visited the club, for a famous comedian visited our club in June 1978, introduced by Albert Dodd. To this day members recall Frank 'it's the way I tell 'em' Carson standing at the bar telling jokes.

CHAPTER ELEVEN

Ladies Golf at Droitwich

LADIES WERE prominent among the founder members of Droitwich Golf Club, there being seven, a quarter of the membership and by 1905 this number had all but doubled. Most were wives of members but some unmarried ladies are listed in teams.

The first record of a ladies competition dates from 1899, when Mrs. Roden won the Final Ladies Monthly Medal with a score of 54 - 12 = 42. She gained further honours in that she was elected to the club's committee in the same year, demonstrating that ladies were already part of the club. This in itself was unusual; the fact that a lady was actually sitting in committee this early must have been unique and is still the exception rather than the rule today.

This suggests that the ladies got away to a happy start at Droitwich and have continued to enjoy their golf throughout the club's history. There have always been fewer ladies than men, except in 1936, when it is rumoured that the ladies actually outnumbered the men! They pay a lower subscription than the men and so their privileges are restricted but there has always been a tradition of mutual respect and courtesy between the sexes which even extends to the pleasant annual match. Moreover, in the matter of keeping minutes, the ladies are definitely superior for theirs predate the mens' by thirty years.

By 1901 the ladies felt ready to engage in a match with another club and on 29th October played the ladies of Worcester. In those days matches were decided on the aggregate number of holes won so the result: Worcester Ladies 19, Droitwich Ladies 0 represented a substantial defeat. Our team was: Miss Hall, Mrs. H. Shirley Jones and the two Miss Tombs. This may have dented their confidence because when the Worcestershire Ladies County Golf Association was formed soon afterwards, Droitwich Ladies declined the invitation to join. However they sent their good wishes for the Association's success. The fixture appears to have been a regular one and in 1908 a Miss Stretton represented the club. She was a cousin of the Miss Stretton who was

Ladies vice-captain in 1929 but was unable to take up office as captain the following year, for she had married the Bromsgrove cricketer Joe Tilt and they produced a son, David. He has a one pint pewter tankard inscribed 'DGC 1928 Mixed Flag JDT & GMJS'. This Miss Stretton was also the first winner of the Droitwich Ladies Challenge Bowl, now know as the Rose Bowl.

The ladies' contribution to the war effort has already been described and it seems that it was not until 1922 that the ladies began to function fully again when Mrs. E. Evans took her place on the committee. As she was the mayor's wife, the links between club and town continued to be fostered. Within three years there were no less than three ladies on the committee, Mrs. Blake, Mrs. W.A. Solven and Mrs. Burgoyne, whose husband also served. It is to the credit of the ladies that they were so well represented on the committee when the club made its most historic step since its foundation - the move to Westford House and the opening of the eighteen hole course.

Another fact pleasant to record is that the wife of the new professional, William Dean, was permitted to play and often represented the club in ladies teams. She won the Rose Bowl in 1931. Such democracy would have been frowned on in many clubs, not merely at that period. A similar courtesy was also extended to Doris Whiting when her brother Len was the professional and on 24th June 1951 she returned a net 62 off a handicap of fourteen. Doris helped in the club kitchen, while her father, Bill, ran the bar and acted as assistant professional. Doris won the Burgoyne Cup three years running in the early fifties and also the Rose Bowl with Mrs. Haigh.

In 1926 the ladies became affiliated to the L.G.U. Mrs. Joyce Holyoake upheld her family's tradition of service to the club when she became secretary of the ladies section in that year. Mrs. W. Kay, long-serving captain in the twenties and thirties, became the first Droitwich member to serve as representative on the county committee. From 1938 Mrs. Kate Neligan performed the same role which she undertook for a number of years until 1952. A forceful character she was Droitwich's leading lady golfer, playing off a handicap of eight becoming ladies' captain in the late thirties. Mrs. Neligan was featured in 'The Leaders in the Spa' series in the Droitwich Guardian. After the war she played less golf but by then her daughter Kitty, who had joined the club in 1933, aged ten, had succeeded her as the ladies' premier golfer.

Being such an important part of the club, with representatives on the committee and prominent townspeople among members and officials it is hardly surprising that ladies' membership continued to rise. From seven in 1897 numbers grew steadily until a ceiling was reached in 1955 when there were no less than seventy two lady members, with the result that in 1973 quotas had to be agreed. These were: 360 full men, 60 full ladies; 100 five day men and 35 five day ladies.

The only pause in this trend had been the second World War, when the club's activities were in abeyance. Once again, the ladies acted with more initiative than the men, Mrs. Joyce Holyoake taking charge of the trophies for safekeeping 'for the duration'. [126]

The L.G.U. recommended that handicaps should be held in abeyance during the hostilities and ladies played off local handicaps when they had the opportunity to do so in any competitions organised by the secretary.

The first meeting after the war was the A.G.M. with Mrs. Holyoake in the chair. She continued as president of the ladies section for another four years, having first taken office in 1936. Mrs. Betty Madin was elected captain and was re-elected annually until 1951. She was a useful golfer who gave valued service to the club, which was recognised by her election as president in the mid-sixties. Miss Dorothy Cartridge continued as secretary and also took on the not very onerous task of looking after the finances, as the bank balance stood at £8.15s. She continued as secretary until 1952, when she was elected captain, a post she held for two years, when she reverted to being a committee member for a further two years. She then stood down as a new rule had been passed requiring people to resign from the committee after a certain period of time to enable newer members to become acquainted with committee work. Her service to the club, which had begun as a committee member in 1934, was recognised by election as president from 1959 until 1965.

Ladies day had been on a Wednesday until 1935, when Thursday became 'their day'. This continued for thirty years when it was changed to Tuesday as Thursday is half day closing in Droitwich and the men wanted to play on their afternoon off. There was a more enlightened approach in 1946, though, because the main committee allowed the ladies to play their competitions on Saturday afternoons in the winter because so many of the fourteen ladies with LGU handicaps were at work during the week.

The ladies section had rejoined the LGU after the war, when the course S.S.S. stood at 72. In 1947 the ladies applied to the LGU for approval to lower this to 70. This was forthcoming and the standard scratch score for ladies remains at that figure despite the alterations to the course.

In 1949 it was felt that the roles of secretary and treasurer should be split and Mrs. Mary Waters took over the financial guidance of the section, a post she held for the next fifteen years. She was the wife of John Waters, a leading light in the men's section for many years and gave him sterling support. She became ladies president in 1967 and remained so for twelve years, when she was made an honorary life member of the club.

When the club became a limited company in the mid 1950's, Mrs. Bill Morgan was invited to become a director, another example of Droitwich Golf Club's enlightened approach. She was a useful golfer and a force in the club for many years, having four terms as captain, the 1961 stint in harness with her husband Les as mens captain. She was president between 1979 and 1981.

Meanwhile, Kate Neligan was back in office during the 1950's, being president for eight years, while daughter Kitty became captain in the mid-fifties for three years, marrying Geoff Bill in 1957 and sharing a few months in office with him when he returned as mens' captain in 1958. Kitty remembers the captaincy as being 'hard work but enjoyable'. It 'didn't have the competitive edge that it has now'. Kitty Bill's lowest handicap, like her mother's was eight, and other ladies attained respectable handicaps, such as Mrs. Doris Colpus, who was secretary of the section from 1951 until 1955 and again in 1959-61.

This was the start of a new era for the Droitwich ladies. Mrs. Joyce Haigh took over as secretary in 1956, by which time there were sixty full playing members of the section, who gave good support to competitions and matches.

Why are the ladies all so happy? Phyl Lambe (captain 1959) is pointing out the reason. Prominent members of the ladies section in this picture include Joyce Haigh, Dorothy Cartridge, Mary Waters, Bill Morgan, Betty Madin and Doris Colpus. The year may be 1958 when Janet Roberts (front row. 4th from right) was captain

It was no longer necessary to play competitions on Saturdays in the winter, but some business ladies were still allowed to play their competitions at weekends. As Mrs. Haigh was also ladies' handicap secretary she had plenty to do. Her first spell as secretary ended in 1958, but she resumed the role in the early sixties, continuing in that capacity for fourteen years. For her long and loyal service, she was made an honorary life member in 1971.

The older ladies who had kept the club going during the '30s and '40s were gradually bowing out and new faces such as those mentioned above were taking over the reins, with the help and encouragement of their seniors and the ever present Miss Cartridge to guide and advise them every step of the way.

Prominent among lady golfers in the 60's was Mrs. Doris Brittain, a good player who won many trophies. She was captain in 1965-6 and again in 1970 and served on the county ladies committee and the county lady veterans committee. The ladies were delighted to have a representative on both committees. Clearly the standard of ladies golf was improving; Kitty Bill recalls, 'In the last twenty years there have been a lot of very good golfers, some of whom have done well in higher grades of golf... prior to that people were unambitious about it, just enjoyed it'. In 1967 the ladies entered a team in the county championship for the first time, but the year was also significant in that it saw the institution of the Goulash Competitions.

This boost to social and competitive golf was initiated by the club captain, Percy Rishworth, who wanted to organise something on Sunday afternoons. The Goulash Competitions were very good as a gentle introduction to competitions for those who were apprehensive and lacked experience and as a means of introducing new members to a wider group. Sometimes as many as thirty participants would enter this mixed foursomes competition. It became a social event and the prizes, bought out of the 30p entrance fee, were golf balls. Albert and Billy Lippett ran them for thirteen years, then Geraldine and Ian Muir, followed by Irene Taylor (ladies' captain 1983 & 1990) who ran them for three years. After Irene, Olive Young (ladies' captain 1976) and her husband, Cyril, took over. The Three-club competition and Family Foursomes probably sprang out of this event. The Goulashes were taken out of the competition calendar in 1989 but restarted in 1995. They are now arranged as and when there is a vacant slot in an increasingly busy calendar.

Miss Gwyneth Presley (later to become Mrs. Presley-Jones) took over from Mrs. Waters as treasurer and gave excellent service until 1985. These two ladies laid a wonderful foundation for the running of the finances of the section. The ladies subscriptions are paid to the club: the income for running the section arises from the Ladies Open, the Harry Whitehouse Mixed Open and competition entry fees.

Mrs. Presley-Jones was a science teacher and apparently a formidable character. 'We were all terrified of her', one lady recalls. Her sporting achievements included success as a runner while at university.

By 1970 the ladies team was good enough to win all its matches including that against the men, an event which began ten years earlier. The ladies rallied round to assist with the catering for the Phoenix Metals Pro-am, foreshadowing the events of 1977, when the club was without a steward. The ladies rallied round once again and organised the catering for the opening of the new holes. They had to clean the kitchens, which were in a terrible state and unfit for the preparation of food. To complicate matters further, there was a bread strike on and Sylvia Gray remembers having to go to the shops at 8.30 a.m. to pick up the loaves that had been ordered. Refreshments were served all day until 11.00 p.m. and Sylvia organised a rota to enable all the volunteers to play in the competition.

The ladies were rewarded for their efforts as when the English Ladies Golf Association in 1972 put a levy of 20p on every playing member of affiliated clubs, the general committee stated that the club would pay the necessary amount as 'the ladies had been so co-operative and worked so hard during the year!' This annual levy is now paid through the subscription.

In 1973 the question arose as to whether the ladies' cups be presented at the annual dinner dance, as usual, or at the ladies dinner. Mrs. Morgan thought that they should be presented at the dinner dance, as if they were not presented then 'the ladies would be retiring more into the background and as it was we were hardly acknowledged as members of the club by many of the men'. It was agreed to follow the normal practice.

In the same year the lady captain asked at a general committee meeting about the removal of stones from the bunkers, only to be told: 'There are no stones in our bunkers!'

The lady captain did not always receive such curt treatment, for in 1974 the general committee agreed that, similar to the men's captain, the lady captain need not pay a subscription during her year of office.

A delightful annual event was instituted in 1975 when Mrs. Margaret Groom presented an old putter as a trophy to be played for by the past lady captains. Up to twenty ladies play and are joined at lunch by other past captains who enjoy meeting old friends and exchanging reminiscences of their own playing days.

For a number of years the only junior lady member playing at Droitwich had been Miss Pauline Cook, now Mrs. Clements. Following a request from the County Ladies Golf Association, the formation of a junior ladies section was mooted, and in 1975 Mrs. Margaret Shaw, who was then captain of the section, took the initiative. She managed to enrol ten girls, including Aileen

108

Gray, daughter of Jim and Sylvia. This encouraged Sylvia Gray to assist Mrs. Shaw and she eventually took over the organisation of the girls. The numbers quickly rose to fifteen, but fluctuated as interest waxed and waned. A number who gave the game up in their teens returned as married ladies and resumed a golfing 'career'. Others found their membership a career advantage in the wider world.

The lady president of the day, Mrs. Mary Waters, presented a cup bearing her name for the best net score on junior day, whilst Mrs. Maud Holm presented the Holm Cup which became the scratch championship trophy. Mrs. Marion Lancaster presented a trophy for a nine hole competition for beginners and Peter Turton presented the Turton Trophy for any girl who put a lot of effort into her golf, without necessarily being the best player.

A major step was taken in 1981 with the inauguration of the Girls Open, the first of its kind in the country, it is believed, which caters for girls of all ages and abilities. This was started by Sylvia and Jim Gray and has grown over the years, a field of seventy seven entering one year. Internationals and beginners have responded to 400 posters sponsored by E.C. Osborne, the stationers, and publicity in the media has helped put Droitwich firmly on the map of girls golf. Many of today's lady professionals played in the open during their formative years, including Helen Dobson (when only ten years old), Suzanne Strudwick, Sarah Nicklin (one of our own girls), Susan Hodge, née Shapcott and her sister Alison.

One of our girls, Angela Cluley, brought national honours to Droitwich by winning the Abraham Trophy at the English Girls Championship in 1992. The format of this particular competition begins with the average of six cards being sent to the county junior organiser. The girls compete in the Midland Girls Championship and the winners go to the national final.

The majority of our girls have played for the county juniors, including Karen Greenfield and Clair

Angela Cluley (on left) receives the National Abraham Trophy from county president, Betty Pryce-Jones, 1992

George, who although no longer members of Droitwich are key members of the county first team.

Madeleine George, who, donated the Girls Open Cup, Ros Weston and Nan Burne followed Sylvia Gray as organisers when Sylvia 'graduated' to run the county girls team.

A number of ladies who were to give distinguished service to the club, both on the course and in official capacities, joined during the 1970's.

The Rev. Marian Talbot joined in 1970 at the same time as Sylvia Gray and they learned their golf together. It was a great regret of Marian that she had to give up her membership in 1979, the year of Sylvia's captaincy, because of the 'unsocial hours' of her work. However she returned ten years later and donned her cassock one day in 1991 to conduct a memorial service for Tich Baylis, leading a solemn procession of 'Salties' to the drinking fountain beside the fifteenth tee, which was dedicated to Tich's memory.

Marian and Sylvia used to play very quickly and once got a ticking off from Isabel Morphy for playing too fast. The Grays joined Droitwich because the atmosphere was more like that to which they had been accustomed in Scotland:

You're all Jock Tamson's bairns up there, it doesn't matter what you are and there is a completely different attitude to golf. When we looked around the clubs down here some of them were obviously on the snobbish side. The main thing about Droitwich is that it is very friendly.

Very soon after settling in Droitwich Sylvia went to pay the butcher. The butcher was the club captain, Ron Wall, and he asked her if her husband played golf. It seems Jim had missed his interview the previous evening, but was accepted anyway. The following Sunday he was playing in the first game in a foursomes match - Jim was playing off seven and had never even played in a team in Scotland as he was not considered good enough off such a high handicap!

Another lady who joined in the 70's with a distinguished golfing pedigree was Ros Weston, whose father, Jack Urry, competed in all four rounds of the Open Championship at St. Andrews in 1946 and became president of the English Golf Union in 1971. She equalled the ladies course record at Droitwich in 1985, the year in which she was captain with a score of seventy-four, holding the record jointly with Sarah Nicklin. This record fell to Simone Morgan in 1994 with 72. In 1992 Ros became captain of the Worcestershire County ladies first team, having been second team captain previously. She considered this not only an honour to herself but a great honour for Droitwich Golf Club. She now serves on the Midlands committee, organising the Midland Ladies Championship. It can be seen that Droitwich ladies have made a huge contribution to county golf in recent years, evidence of the continually improving standard of golf and the dedication and commitment to the organisation of the game by a number of determined ladies, including Marion Lancaster, Sylvia Gray and Jenny Harrison who ran the county for two years when Ros was captain.

It was therefore something of shock to the system when in 1984, one lady felt moved to write to the ladies secretary:

I am writing because I feel we should take seriously the remarks made by a gentleman member at the recent AGM concerning congestion on the 1st tee on Saturday mornings. I am afraid it will only take one proposition by one of the considerable number of 'anti-lady' members at the next AGM for our playing times to be restricted further, possibly in line with clubs like Harborne and Blackwell where ladies are not allowed on the course at weekends until after 4 p.m.... I know the excellent relationship which we enjoy at Droitwich with our general committee is the envy of a good many other ladies sections.

It was the Droitwich ladies who pioneered a new Handicap League in 1984 in which a number of Worcestershire clubs compete for a trophy presented by Droitwich ladies.

The next season was only the third in which Karen Cheetham had played golf, but she was already good enough to be selected for the county second team. She did even better in 1986, winning the Worcestershire ladies championship at Blackwell, beating the more experienced Jenny Deeley in the semi-final in the morning. The final, against Janice Kerr of Redditch, was not without a few scares. A thinned chip-shot on the thirteenth, apparently destined for a brook, rolled over a bridge and enabled Karen to chip back from dry ground. Her opponent, on the green in two, having observed Miss Cheetham's recovery, took three more to get down - match all square. With the considerable support of her caddy, Sylvia Gray, Karen then went on to win and was awarded her county colours the same year.

Karen Cheetham (on right) receives the Worcestershire Ladies Championship Trophy from county captain Sheila Marshall at Blackwell, 1986

In 1988 Droitwich ladies joined the newly formed Midland Scratch League with some confidence also winning the Gross Team Trophy in the Worcestershire County Championships in the same year. The team was K. Bendle, S. Gray, K. Greenfield, J. Harrison and

111

R. Weston. Scratch League success followed in 1989 when the ladies were promoted to Division One, which they won the following year, the team being M. Archer, C. George,   K. Greenfield, J. Harrison, C. Mayneord, L. Mitchell and R. Weston.

On a lighter note, in the hard winter of 1988 Helen Rowley's ball came to rest on the frozen surface of the pond on the sixth. Not sure if it would count as a dropped shot if she picked the ball off the ice, Helen elected to play the ball as it lay: 'it was a magnificent shot which landed on the green'.[127]

At present there are two ladies with single figure handicaps. Jenny Harrison off 6 who, in 1981 scored a gross 71 in the Harry Whitehouse Mixed Open with the help of her husband Charles, and Margaret Archer off 8.

Margaret tied for Midland Golfer of the year in 1992 at Kings Norton but lost the play-off on the second extra hole to a birdie. Three years later Margaret was again runner-up. Clair George also kept Droitwich to the fore in 1993 by qualifying for the last thirty two of the English Match Play and Strokeplay events, held at St. Enodoc and Kings Norton respectively. This was a remarkable year for the ladies because they won the Handicap League, The Scratch League and the County Team Championship, M. Archer, H. Cocks, C. George, J. Harrison and R. Weston representing the club.

The Ladies County Championship was played at Droitwich in that year, Clair George being the Runner-up.

Recognition of the ladies success resulted in the general committee deciding to restrict the use of the course to ladies only until twelve noon on Tuesdays, despite the opposition of the five day members, who said that although they had paid their subscriptions for five days play they now only had four and a half.

In an afterword to 'A History of Golf in Britain' published in 1952, Lord Brabazon of Tara wrote:

The trouble is that so many golf clubs will not cater for the girls - for the women it is not a very pleasant thing to go down to some golf clubs where women are looked upon as almost a weed or excrescence which is not required anywhere near the place. Many clubs have that outlook on life, and if women are not going to be welcome at golf clubs they are not going to allow their men to go there... the club has got to be a social thing with women there so that everybody can find amusement... But if you look upon the whole thing as something which is only for men as it was twenty years ago, then your club is as good as dead.

None of this can be said to apply to Droitwich, which for one hundred years has set a standard for all clubs to aspire to in its treatment of the ladies. In return the ladies of Droitwich have made their mark indelibly on ladies golf.

CHAPTER TWELVE

The Seniors

'THE GOLFER *is never old until he is decrepit. So long as providence allows him the use of two legs, active enough to carry him round the greens, and of two arms supple enough to take a 'half swing', there is no reason why his enjoyment of the game need be seriously diminished'.   (The Rt. Hon. Arthur Balfour)* [128]

THE SENIORS section was founded by A.V. Brackston in the late sixties. They used to play on Wednesday afternoons and there were sixteen in a team. They had fixtures against the senior sections of other clubs including Broadway and Stourbridge. Bill Dowding was eventually elected captain of the section and among the early members were Percy Harris and Len Hartle.

Brackie kept a fatherly eye on things and in his position as club secretary had little difficulty in reserving the first tee for an hour or so for home matches.

The section was refounded on 28th October, 1978, when thirty two members attended a meeting chaired by the club captain, Ray Woodhead. The secretary, Ray Baldwin, addressed the meeting, saying 'it was only to be run on informal lines, the main essential was to create good, old-fashioned fun and an enjoyable pastime for all members to get together and enjoy each others company'. Phil Edwards was elected captain of the seniors in 1978 and at the seniors' A.G.M. of 1995 he was made an honorary life member of the section. John 'Robbie' Robinson was elected secretary, Bill Dowding, chairman and regular committee meetings were held, at which planned programmes of events comprising internal competitions and inter club matches were arranged.

It should be noted, though, that a general committee minute of 25th May, 1977 reads 'It was reported that a senior section had been formed with Mr. Robinson in charge'. Presumably the 1978 meeting was called to place a popular idea on a more formal footing.

By this time the section's membership had grown to thirty two and it continued to rise annually until in 1996 there were no less than 109 members. Whilst companionship has remained one of the key elements of the section the extent of golf being played under the senior umbrella has inevitably made its activities as a whole more significant in relation to the club. This could have created problems but such potential difficulties have been recognised and resolved, often in discussion with club officials and committees.

Up to 1990 the results of the seniors' monthly medals were not assessed by the club's competitions committee but were nevertheless used within the section to adjust unofficial senior handicaps, which were used only in internal senior competitions and matches. This practice, not unique to Droitwich seniors, gave rise to some confusion culminating in an occasion when one of the section involved in an away match asked his partner 'which handicap do we play off today?' The pair in question succeeded in winning their match by a substantial margin and it was not surprising that Droitwich received a sharp letter from the other club involved, wishing to know what all this alternative handicapping was about.

The outcome of this, following discussions with the competitions committee, was a change of status of the monthly medal/stableford events, making these qualifying competitions eligible for handicap adjustments. The unofficial handicaps were discontinued. The yearly programme now includes twenty six matches (two of the most keenly fought being with Droitwich ladies), monthly stroke play events in the summer months (played off the white tees), an annual individual match-play knock-out and a winter league.

Members of Droitwich (not necessarily members of the senior section) have acquitted themselves with some distinction in senior open competitions throughout the midlands in recent years.

Droitwich was one of the first clubs in the midlands to inaugurate an open competition for senior golfers. The Vintage Shield, open to men sixty-five and over was first played in 1968, before the formal establishment of the senior section. This trophy was donated by Jack Rodger who also deposited £100 to be awarded to the first player in this competition to achieve a gross medal score lower than his age in years. This award remained unclaimed until 1995 when John Tyson, a Droitwich senior, shot a gross 84 at the age of eighty-five. This was a rare occasion for the club as the Vintage winner was Alan Rees with John Tyson second and Jim Gray third - all members of the home club.

Jack Rodger joined the club in 1964, having moved down from Glasgow with his wife Marjorie. Both were keen and good golfers, having played at Cathkin Braes in Glasgow. Jack presented the Vintage Shield in memory of a

114

feat of his father's, who was a founder member of Cathkin Braes. He died in 1976, aged 76.

John Tyson is a quiet man and professes embarrassment at the size of his prize. Even so he was hoping to repeat the achievement the following year. He regularly acts as starter for county events, spending a whole day on the first tee even in the most inclement weather.

The oldest regularly playing member of the seniors is Bob Goodall who was born in 1908. He started playing golf at the Lickey Hills course when he was 65, through his membership of Probus. He came to Droitwich about ten years ago. He was a third generation employee of the Great Western Railway until the fall of the Beeching axe, when he became a buyer for the East Worcestershire Waterworks Company.

John Weston's uncle George Cowper is a year older than Bob. He plays less frequently however, but was recently spotted hitting balls on the practice field when a few months short of his 90th birthday! A former accountant and stockbroker, he has been a member of Droitwich since the late 50's.

The seniors represent an important section of our club and enjoy their matches and competitions with considerable enthusiasm.

CHAPTER THIRTEEN

The Centenary and Beyond

W E LOOK to history not only to relate the past but also to explain how the present state of affairs came about. Whilst it is the early history which brought Droitwich Golf Club into being and enabled it to survive and to prosper through and beyond two world wars the last twenty years has done much to shape the course and the character of the club as we now know it.

There have been two occasions in recent years when there was a possibility of a major change in the scope of the club. In 1991 there appeared a distinct prospect of the land to the east of Crutch Lane being re-zoned for residential development. Interest was expressed by a number of housing developers and the potential money involved would have more than covered the cost of purchasing land and laying out new holes together with a new clubhouse to the west of Crutch Lane and to the north of the present boundary of the course. In the event the local authority opted to open up areas for further housing to the south of the town and this issue never materialised.

More recently, in 1994, following the death of the owner of Ford Farm we were offered at a favourable price eighty five acres (or should we say thirty four hectares?) at £1,800 per acre on the opposite side of Ford Lane which would have afforded the opportunity for a new loop of nine holes. The purchase and development of this land would have had to be funded by the club itself. The proposal to go ahead with this project was rejected by the membership at an EGM on 13th December 1994 although the voting was 96 to 55 in favour this did not provide the percentage majority required by the company's rules. There was some concern about the problems of drainage and, perhaps, a substantial body of the members felt that a major ongoing financial commitment for something which would take some years to be of real benefit was not desirable.

The fact that these major projects did not materialise did not deter the club from recognising the need for bringing the course and its facilities up to a standard commensurate with the dawn of the twenty first century and the enhanced standing of Droitwich in the county scene. In keeping with this positive spirit the proposal to undertake a major redevelopment of part of the clubhouse was wholeheartedly supported. The fact that this coincided with the club's centenary may have been fortuitous but the level of enthusiasm surely reflected a sense that this was a fine way to mark the occasion.

Although there has been no single outlay of capital comparable with the clubhouse extension there has been no holding back on expenditure in improving the course and providing major items of new machinery which are not only labour saving but have also contributed to the excellent condition of the greens and fairways which are recognised to be amongst the best in the county. Since the change to two loops of nine some twenty years ago, comprehensive planting of trees, mostly grown from saplings and subsequently relocated, has transformed the appearance and character of many holes. These groups of mature trees interspersed along many fairways have provided legitimate penalties for the wayward shots and represent a much more satisfactory solution than the areas of heavy rough they replaced. The course as a whole has acquired some considerable character and is a pleasant place to be when one pauses for a moment without, of course, holding up play.

The Kays multistory warehouse on the industrial estate is the only blot on the landscape and even this is hardly obtrusive when all the trees are in full leaf.

In playing terms A, B, C, seniors and ladies teams all have extensive programmes of matches against other clubs. The monthly medal competitions for men are supplemented by a number of other annual competitions most of which are played for specific cups donated to the club over the years. The ladies have a comprehensive calendar of events and the mixed competitions are extremely popular. In addition to these formal events there are several informal groups within the club which organise ad hoc competitions. This says something about the attitude to the game within the membership. There is a general air of healthy competition and the standard of golf is certainly above average.

Overall the course and the club itself have matured well and this must reflect much credit on the diligence and imagination of the officers and committee members. The decision to have a post of chairman rather than president has proved most beneficial and we have been fortunate in having a series of chairmen who have given positive guidance to the development of the club whilst allowing the various committees to get on with their particular tasks.

Preparations for the centenary got under way early. The 200 club was set up and John Bromhead was asked to write this book. No one could have

117

imagined just what his painstaking investigations would reveal. As time has progressed all sections of the club have set about planning their programmes for 1997 under the umbrella of the main committee. Members may not appreciate how much time and effort have been put in to making this a year to remember. The ladies section has been particularly active and innovative both in raising money to fund events and in making Droitwich the venue for an annual competition of the Blind Golfers Association in addition to their own internal programme of events. They have also provided a permanent memento of the occasion in the form of a tapestry showing the clubhouse before the 1996 extension, viewed from the ninth green. The idea of a tapestry originated from the ladies centenary committee, who asked Helen Godber to design and plan the project. She co-ordinated this magnificent effort, which took two years to complete, with over 60 ladies actively involved.

The most permanent feature of the centenary year must be the new wing on the clubhouse, the biggest single investment since the club moved to Ford Lane in 1923. It is hoped that we shall have lots of sunny days ahead so that members can sit on the balcony at the end of their round and survey happenings on the first and tenth tees and on the ninth and eighteenth greens. Perhaps even the old members who have finally hung up their clubs will find this a delightful spot from which to observe and reminisce. On the social front the Centenary gala function will be the highlight but there will be numerous other occasions to mark 1997 as not just any old year. It is hoped to arrange exchange visits with Dieppe-Pourville golf club which is also having its centenary in 1997.

The centenary marks a milestone in the history of the club. Its survival and growth through two world wars, despite the decline of Droitwich as a health resort, has been quite an achievement. Several Worcestershire clubs established at about the same time have ceased to exist. There is no doubt that there were difficult times and the gradual change in membership from one based on professional gentlemen and their ladies to a wider cross section of the community has taken place remarkably smoothly and has resulted in a friendly club with few, if any, cliques. There may well be a parallel with the change in the character of Droitwich itself which is no longer the inland spa resort of the pre-war years but has increased in population boosted by overspill from Birmingham and has experienced the growth of several light industrial and service enterprises.

In financial terms the club has managed itself well over the years with the help of local benefactors in the early days but subsequently due to the dedication and competence of elected officials supported by the good sense and commitment of the membership. In the 80s and 90s there has been enormous growth in golfing activity and this expanding market has been met by the development of new golf courses and complexes. Many of these, however, are essentially commercial enterprises owned in part or totally by a single landowner or a business company and the membership, as such, has little control and often limited influence on policy matters or the running of the club.

To what extent do we have to compete with these rival enterprises? Droitwich is owned by its membership and long may this continue. There are always temptations to expand and develop and even embrace other sporting activities. When these issues have arisen the membership has taken a cautious view perhaps seeing the dangers of increased overheads or interest on major borrowing necessitating such an income contribution from visitors, particularly societies, that they would begin to have priority over the use of the course and the clubhouse.

To an extent the past shapes the future. As is evident in the preceding chapters, changes in society itself and in the character of the town of Droitwich have greatly influenced the development of the club. However, it is perhaps unwise to be fatalistic and to suppose that the club can do nothing to alter the course of events which future historians will recount.

What the future will bring is hard to predict in this age of rapid and radical change. If the political pundits are right and another four million new houses are needed in the next twenty years is it likely that the five holes east of Crutch lane will again be sought as building land? The present view of the powers that be, and this surely reflects the hopes of the membership, is that the character of the club should not change, the course should continue to suit the average player, the membership numbers should stay at about the present level and there should be no increased dependence on visiting societies to augment the income. There will, doubtless, be more use of the extended clubhouse for social activities within the club.

It is fun to speculate. Can one visualise a time when fossil fuels run out and personal transport is limited to an electric buggy? Golf will surely not be superseded by wearing a headset and getting virtual reality on the computer. So will everyone live in walking distance of the first tee surrounded by energy efficient residential homes? Will the club become the normal eating out place and will it have its own corner shop and post office? Perhaps not an altogether unpleasant prospect.

There have been some memorable characters associated with the club either as active members, staff or as benefactors. Paternalism has given way to sponsorship and the days when a club could depend for its income on a relatively small number of well-to-do members have long gone. Do we still have such characters or their equivalent today or is political correctness turning us all into uniformly ungracious but just considerate enough zombies? Are we seeing the beginning of 'partner hugging' and 'rough rage' as the acceptable exhibitions of joy at winning and agony at drifting off the fairway? The next century is looking interesting!

Epilogue

We've penned for your pleasure
    The facts of past days,
When members at leisure
    Played golf on the Bays.

Our forbears were they,
    Both ladies and gents,
Who went out to play
    In those far off events.

With that hickory shaft
    And with gutties to boot
Oh, they must have been daft
    To suppose they could shoot

A respectable score
    By the standards we know,
But in those days of yore
    They were having their go.

Not for us is to doubt
    Their love of the game,
Year in and year out
    Plus ça change c'est the same.

From the Bays to Ford Lane
    That really made news
With so much to gain
    And so little to lose.

As the course was expanded
    To eighteen full holes
Finances demanded
    More misguided souls

Should buy a few clubs.
    What of slices and hooks,
If they first pay their subs
    So to balance the books?

To two loops of nine,
    In an effort to please,
Most thought it just fine
    But that hole through the trees

On the top of the hill;
    Were we told it was moving?
Why can't we stand still
    And stop this improving?

Round that dam' Hawthorn hedge
    To the green on hole twelve,
Two woods and a wedge,
    If we're lucky: please shelve

All these things, which may well
    Make our course a bit longer,
But, as age starts to tell,
    We get weaker not stronger.

It ever was thus,
    Through those one hundred years,
That the members would fuss
    And give vent to their fears

That the future is never
    As good as the past;
May now be forever
    And this change be the last.

Officers of Droitwich Golf Club

Club Captains

1897	Dr. H. Shirley Jones	1946	E.R. Fabricius	1972	I. Bedford
1898	"	1947	G.C.H. Bill	1973	B.M Joule
1899	"	1948	"	1974	A.J. Hawes
1900	"	1949	A.A. Roberts	1975	P.R.S. Pessol
1901	"	1950	G.C.H. Bill	1976	A.C. Ives
1902	The Rev. F.D. Richardson	1951	J.A. Waters	1977	C.W. Davies
1903	"	1952	"	1978	R. Woodhead
1905	"	1953	"	1979	P.A. Turton
1906	"	1954	"	1980	R.G. Tunstall
1907	"	1955	"	1981	B. Tomkins
1908	Capt. F.A.W. How	1956	T.W. Moffatt	1982	A.E. Cox
1921	The Rev. F.D. Richardson	1957	S.P. Haynes	1983	A.E. Lippett
1922	"	1958	G.C.H. Bill	1984	J. Gray
1923	Howard L. Green	1959	H.C. Hill	1985	J. S. Struthers
1924	"	1960	W.T. Lamb	1986	C.R.J. Harrison
1925	"	1961	I.W. Morgan	1987	R.J. Carter
1926	"	1962	N.L. Baker	1988	J.A.F. Mole
1927	"	1963	"	1989	B.D. Bishop
1928	"	1964	R.H. Whitehouse	1990	A.B. Harrington
1929	J.S. Burgoyne	1965	W.F. Best	1991	G.E. Hudspith
1930	F.W.E. Sharples	1966	D.J. Walsh	1992	C.N. Brade
1936	"	1967	P.J. Rishworth	1993	R.I. Mayneord
1937	"	1968	T.F. Ashenden	1994	D.A. Fellows
1938	C. Osborn	1969	H.B. Cartwright	1995	T.R. Bourne
1939	"	1970	R. Wall	1996	I.J. Rone
1940	"	1971	H.B. Gilmore	1997	W.W. Jarvis

Lady Captains

1902	Mrs. F.D. Richardson	1958	Mrs. J.P. Roberts	1979	Mrs. S.B. Gray
1903	"	1959	Mrs. P. Lamb	1980	Mrs. J. Harvey
1928	Mrs. W. Kay	1960	Mrs. E.A. Morgan	1981	Mrs. M.I. George
1929	"	1961	"	1982	Mrs. M. Lancaster
1936	Mrs. J.M. Holyoake	1962	Mrs. K.J. Bill	1983	Mrs. I. Taylor
1937	Mrs. W. Kay	1963	Mrs. V. Best	1984	Mrs. M. Somerville
1938	Mrs. K.M.L. Neligan	1964	Mrs. E.A. Morgan	1985	Mrs. R.M. Weston
1939	"	1965	Mrs. D.M. Brittain	1986	Mrs. J. Harrison
1940	"	1966	"	1987	Mrs. P.V. Tattersall
1946	Miss E. Madin	1967	Mrs. M.S. Jeffery	1988	Mrs. E.M. Jones
1947	"	1968	"	1989	Mrs. C.N. Burne
1948	"	1969	Mrs. B.M. Holm	1990	Mrs. I. Taylor
1949	"	1970	Mrs. D.M. Brittain	1991	Rev. M. Talbot
1950	"	1971	Mrs. D.V. Hill	1992	Mrs. A.M. Price
1951	"	1972	Mrs. M. J. Groom	1993	Mrs. C. Mayneord
1952	Miss C.D. Cartridge	1973	Mrs. M. Milligan	1994	Mrs. L.K. Ottway
1953	"	1974	Mrs. E.A. Morgan	1995	Mrs. N. Williams
1954	Mrs. E.A. Morgan	1975	Mrs. M. Shaw	1996	Mrs. P. Bradley
1955	Miss K.J. Neligan	1976	Mrs. O. Young	1997	Mrs. S.B. Gray
1956	"	1977	Mrs. E.M. Jones		
1957	"	1978	Mrs. J.A. Phillips		

Presidents

1897-1901	J. Corbett		1973-1974	H. Hill
1901-1906	Dr. T. Corbett		1974-1975	G.C.H. Bill
1907	J.W. Spencer		1975-1976	P.J. Rishworth
1921-1922	Lord Doverdale		1976-1977	L.W. Morgan
(the 1st Baron)			1977-1978	N.L. Baker
1946-1949	Lord Doverdale		1978-1979	W.F. Best
(the 3rd Baron)			1979-1980	D.J. Walsh
1950-1970	J.R. Hugh Sumner C.B.E.		1980-1981	R. Wall
1971-1972	J.A. Waters		1981	J. Gray
1972-1973	A.V. Brackston			

Chairmen

1981-1983	J. Gray		1988-1991	B.M. Joule
1983-1985	P.A. Hughes C.B.E., D.F.C.		1991-1994	C.W. Davies
1985-1988	R.G. Tunstall		1994-	G.E. Hudspith

Lady Presidents

1936-1949	Mrs J.M. Holyoake		1981-1983	Mrs B.J. Haigh
1950-1958	Mrs K.M.L. Neligan		1983-1988	Mrs O.N. Young
1959-1965	Miss C.D. Cartridge		1988-1991	Mrs J.A. Phillips
1965-1967	Miss E. Madin		1991-1994	Mrs E.M. Jones
1967-1979	Mrs M. Waters		1994-1996	Mrs N. Burne
1979-1981	Mrs E.A. Morgan		1996-	Mrs M. Lancaster

Honorary Life Members

G.C.H. Bill	Mrs. B.J. Haigh
J.A. Waters	D. J. Walsh
L.W. Morgan	R.J.W. Baldwin
Mrs. M. Waters	J.E. Bickerton Jnr
H.M. Macdonald	

Principal Trophy Winners

Club Championship

1972	G. Shinton	1981	A.J. Terry	1990	D.B. Nevett
1973	J.S. Struthers	1982	D. Eddiford	1991	D. Glover
1974	J.S. Struthers	1983	D. Eddiford	1992	N. Wood
1975	G. Shinton	1984	B. Allen	1993	N. Wood
1976	P. Handy	1985	D.B. Nevett	1994	A.J. Terry
1977	A.J. Terry	1986	J.E. Bickerton	1995	D.B. Nevett
1978	J.S. Struthers	1987	A.W. Bourne	1996	S. Braithwaite
1979	W.B. Owen	1988	J. Bickerton Jnr		
1980	A.J. Terry	1989	S. Braithwaite		

Stroke Play Cup

1973	J.G. Swift	1981	M. Butcher	1989	J. Bickerton Jnr
1974	G. Shinton	1982	A.J. Terry	1990	J. Bickerton Jnr
1975	C.N. Brade	1983	D.J. Eddiford	1991	J. Bickerton Jnr
1976	R.K. Green	1984	D.J. Eddiford	1992	M. Cocks
1977	A. Calkeld	1985	A.J. Terry	1993	N. Wood
1978	A.J. Terry	1986	D.J. Eddiford	1994	S. Braithwaite
1979	W.B. Owen	1987	A.J. Terry	1995	S. Braithwaite
1980	A.J. Terry	1988	J. Bickerton Jnr	1996	A.J. Terry

Eric Griffin Trophy

1966	P.W. Clements	1969	B.M. Joule	1972	D.J. Walsh
1967	J. Bourne	1970	J. Mole	1973	J.G. Swift
1968	R.K. Green	1971	A.R. Morris	1974	G. Shinton

Eric Griffin Trophy (continued)

1975	W.T. Tansley	1983	D.J. Eddiford	1991	G. Sambrook
1976	T. Dewar	1984	R.C. Lyons	1992	M. Cocks
1977	W.T. Tansley	1985	D. Painter	1993	N.P. Wood
1978	T.P. Stanton	1986	R. Mellor	1994	S. Braithwaite
1979	D.J. Eddiford	1987	M. Hawley	1995	K.J. Prokopowycz
1980	A.J. Terry	1988	J. Bickerton Jnr	1996	G. Sambrook
1981	M. Butcher	1989	D.B. Nevett		
1982	A.J. Terry	1990	K.J. Prokopowycz		

The Secretary's Cup

1967	R.J. Ward	1978	J.E. Bickerton	1988	M.J. Clews
1969	W. Ross	1979	V.R. Reece	1989	S. Kings
1970	J. Ottley	1980	M. Miles	1990	T.K. Bourne
1971	A. Taylor	1981	J. King	1991	C.K. Cutler
1972	P. May	1982	B.L. Hart	1992	S. Shuck
1973	D.J. Barton	1983	P.J. Lancaster	1993	J.E. Troth
1974	R.M. Perry	1984	A.W. Gilbert	1994	S.N. Boroughs
1975	J.A. Ord	1985	J.E. Bickerton	1995	D. Hodgson
1976	I. Muir	1986	R. Allies	1996	A.L. Wood
1977	S.P. Hemming	1987	S. Lees		

Raven Bowl

1949	H.C. Hill	1957	R.K. Green	1965	E.T. Underhill
1950	R.H. Whitehouse	1958	J. Duggan	1966	R.K. Green
1951	J.H. Brackston	1959	R. Chance	1967	N.L. Baker
1952	A.V. Brackston	1960	J. Duggan	1968	R. Vitty
1953	A. Williams	1961	H.G. Green	1969	I.E. Bedford
1954	A.E. Hadley	1962	R. Chance	1970	C.T. Pratt
1955	H. Greenway	1963	D. Renfrew	1971	R.K. Green
1956	W.D. Bryn Thomas	1964	P.W. Clements	1972	I.M. Smith

1973	C. Avern	1981	J. Whitehead	1989	I.J. Rone
1974	W.H. Jefferies	1982	H. Grundy	1990	D. Randle
1975	C.W. Davies	1983	S. Evans	1991	M. Wallis
1976	J. Tyson	1984	M.A. Harrington	1992	G.E. Hudspith
1977	H.T. Leaning	1985	M.J. Clews	1993	G. Bourne
1978	W.L. Harvey	1986	R.S. Burnett	1994	D.H. Cook
1979	N.A. Orton	1987	A.R. Bishop	1995	M.J. Perry
1980	D. Collins	1988	J. Cox	1996	M.A. Harrington

Howard Green Challenge Cup

1922	F. Holyoake	1952	C.F. Everton	1975	T.L. Kendall
1923	Jos. Elvins	1953	G. McDougall	1976	P. Handy
1924	Howard Green	1954	A.E. Hadley	1977	R.K. Green
1925	Howard Green	1955	E.B. Willis	1978	E.J. Eddiford
1926	John Elvins	1956	R.K. Green	1979	A.J. Terry
1927	P.H. Poulton	1957	R.K. Green	1980	H. Grundy
1928	H. Ashforth	1958	J. Duggan	1981	J. Gray
1929	J.S. Burgoyne	1959	R. Sparks	1982	A.J. Terry
1930	R. Spencer Broadley	1960	B. Cullimore	1983	A.J. Terry
1931	Leonard R. Hunt	1961	P.R. Harris	1984	R.C. Lyons
1932	John Green	1962	P. Eastwood	1985	R.B. Bishop
1933	Howard L. Green	1963	J. Duggan	1986	P. Daniels
1934	A.W. Speed	1964	R.K. Green	1987	S. Braithwaite
1935	Clifford Osborn	1965	B. Skillern	1988	J. Cox
1936	R. Wallace	1966	J. Tyson	1989	C.J. Phillips
1937	R.D. Hunter	1967	R.K. Green	1990	R.B. Bishop
1938	A.W. Speed	1968	P.W. Clements	1991	I.R. Dix
1946	G.C.H. Bill	1969	R.K. Green	1992	D.W. Meynell
1947	G. McDougall	1970	R.K. Green	1993	I.R. Dix
1948	W. Davies	1971	M.J. Shaw	1994	A.J. Terry
1949	D.B. Cooksey	1972	P.W. Clements	1995	D.B. Nevett
1950	F. Williamson	1973	P. May	1996	A.J. Terry
1951	R.H. Whitehouse	1974	G. Shinton		

Ladies Club Championship

1983	Miss S. Nicklin	1988	Mrs. J. Harrison	1993	Mrs. M. Archer
1984	Mrs. J. Harrison	1989	Mrs. M. Archer	1994	Mrs. M. Archer
1985	Mrs. R. Weston	1990	Mrs. G. Muir	1995	Miss C. George
1986	Mrs. J. Harrison	1991	Mrs. M. Archer	1996	Mrs. M. Archer
1987	Mrs. J. Harrison	1992	Miss C. George		

Burgoyne Cup

1935	Dr. K. Davies-Thomas/ Mrs. Phillips	1961	Mrs. Bill	1979	Mrs. E.M. Jones
		1962	Mrs. Morgan	1980	Mrs. G. Presley-Jones
1936	Mrs. Kay	1963	Miss Madin	1981	Mrs. J.A. Phillips
1937	Mrs. B.K. Harris	1964	Mrs. Rishworth	1982	Mrs. J. Harrison
1938	Mrs. B.K. Harris	1965	Mrs. Bill	1983	Miss K. Cheetham
1939	Mrs. B.K. Harris	1966	Mrs. Brittain	1984	Miss K. Cheetham
1949	Mrs. Morgan	1967	Mrs. Bill	1985	Mrs. M. Nolan
1950	Miss Whiting	1968	Mrs. Bill	1986	Mrs. E. Reece
1951	Miss Whiting	1969	Mrs. Morgan	1987	Mrs. M.L. Archer
1952	Miss Whiting	1970	Mrs. Morgan	1988	Mrs. P. Meredith
1953	Mrs. Hancocks	1971	Mrs. Morgan	1989	Mrs. J. Harvey
1954	Mrs. Morgan	1972	Mrs Presley-Jones	1990	Mrs. S. Gray
1955	Mrs. J.P. Roberts	1973	Mrs. Brittain	1991	Mrs. D. Harrington
1956	Miss K.J. Neligan	1974	Mrs. Brittain	1992	Mrs. C. Mayneord
1957	Mrs. Fildes	1975	Mrs. Morgan	1993	Miss H. Cocks
1958	Miss Madin	1976	Mrs. Burne	1994	Mrs. M. Lightfoot
1959	Mrs. Lamb	1977	Mrs. Coe	1995	Mrs. M. Lightfoot
1960	Miss Kendal	1978	Mrs. R.M. Weston	1996	Mrs. M. Lightfoot

Rose Bowl

1928	Miss M. Stretton	1957	Mrs. Lamb & Miss Cartridge	1974	Mrs. Brittain
1929	Mrs. F.R. Davis			1975	Mrs. Clements
1930	Mrs. Williams	1958	Mrs. Bill & Mrs Hayward	1976	Mrs. Clemens
1931	Mrs. Dean			1977	Mrs. G.M. Muir
1932	Mrs. Kay	1959	Miss Madin & Mrs. Moffat	1978	Mrs. J.A. Phillips
1933	Mrs. Dean			1979	Mrs. K.M. Bendle
1934	Miss C.E. Brazier	1960	Mrs. Morgan & Mrs. Kendal	1980	Mrs. K.M. Bendle
1935	Mrs. Neligan			1981	Miss S. Nicklin
1936	Mrs. Spreckley	1961	Mrs. Morgan & Mrs. Haigh	1982	Mrs. K.M. Bendle
1937	Miss C.E. Brazier			1983	Miss S. Nicklin
1938	Mrs. Kay	1962	Mrs. Morgan & Mrs Stevens	1984	Mrs. R. Weston
1939	Miss P. Corbett			1985	Mrs. R. Weston
1947	Mrs. Tyler	1963	Mrs. Lamb & Mrs. Garrad	1986	Miss K. Cheetham
1951	Mrs. Tyler & Miss Bryant			1987	Mrs. R. Weston
		1964	Mrs. Lamb & Mrs. Rishworth	1988	Mrs. J. Harrison
1952	Mrs. Haigh & Miss Whiting	1965	Mrs. Bill	1989	Mrs. M. Archer
		1966	Mrs. Bill	1990	Mrs. M. Archer
1953	Mrs. Morgan & Mrs. Williams	1967	Mrs. Bill	1991	Miss C. George
		1968	Mrs. Brittain	1992	Mrs. M. Archer
1954	Mrs. Tyler & Mrs. Williams	1969	Mrs. Bunting	1993	Mrs. M. Archer
		1970	Mrs. Brittain	1994	Miss C. George
1955	Mrs. Morgan & Mrs Tyler	1971	Mrs. Brittain	1995	Miss C. George
		1972	Mrs. Brittain	1996	Mrs. M. Archer
1956	Mrs. Fildes & Mrs Preece	1973	Mrs. Brittain		

Bibliography

Primary Sources

Droitwich Golf & Country Club Ltd. Minutes & Archives

Droitwich Golf & Country Club Ltd. Ladies Section Minutes & Archives

Books and Pamphlets

John Behrend *The Amateur*, Droitwich, 1995

Lyn Blewitt & Bob Field *Droitwich - a Pictorial History*, Chichester, 1994

Trevor Boliver *South Staffordshire Golf Club 1892-1992*, [Stafford], 1992

David Cadney *The Story of Olton Golf Club*, Droitwich, 1991

Corbett Estate Offices *Droitwich* [Undated pamphlet]

Richard Darlington & Eric Davey *A Round of a 100 Years - History of Aberdovey Golf Club*, Aberystwyth, 1986

Bernard Darwin *Golf between Two Wars*, London, 1944

Bernard Darwin *The World that Fred Made*, London, 1955

F. Donaldson *P.G. Wodehouse - A Biography*, London, 1982

Droitwich and District Snooker League Handbook 1994/95

Peter Fry *The Whitcombes*, Droitwich, 1994

Ernest Gaskell *Worcestershire Leaders: Social and Political*, London, (1920)

Golfers' Companion, London 1937

Bruce Haley *The Healthy Body and Victorian Culture*, Beknap Press , 1978

H.A. Harris *Sport in Greece and Rome*, London, 1972

Peter Heath *Towards 100 Years*, Droitwich, 1986

Graeme Hick *My Early Life*, London, 1991

A History of Golf in Britain, London, 1952

Michael Hobbs *British Open Champions*, London, 1991

Richard Holt *Stanmore Golf Club 1893-1993. A Social History*, London & Berwick upon Tweed, 1993

Col. A.V. Holyoake *Dear Little Droitwich*, Droitwich, 1977

John Lowerson *Sport and the English Middle Classes 1870-1914*, Manchester, 1993

Lewine Mair *One Hundred Years of Women's Golf*, Edinburgh, 1992

Books and Pamphlets cont.

Clifford Mansfield *100 Years of Golf in Glossop*, [Glossop] 1994

Tony Mason Ed. *Sport in Britain*, Cambridge, 1989

Barbara Middlemass and Joe Hunt *John Corbett Pillar of Salt 1817-1901*, Droitwich 1985

Nikolaus Pevsner *Worcestershire (The Buildings of England)*, London, 1968

Peter Ricketts *The Road to Weatheroak*, Droitwich, 1992

The Royal and Ancient Book of Golf Records, London, 1991

Victoria History of the County of Worcestershire. London, 1906

David Vincent *A History of Evesham Golf Club 1894-1994*, [Evesham], 1994

Clifford Webb *Stourbridge Golf Club Centenary 1892-1992*, Stourbridge, 1992

Miss Enid Wilson *Women's Golf*, (In *A History of Golf in Britain Part II*, London, 1952 pp222-245)

P.G. Wodehouse with Guy Bolton *Bring on the Girls*, London, 1954

Unpublished Books and Documents

A.V. Brackston's Notes

Professor David Wightman's archives

Articles

Birmingham Gazette 20/2/1933

Bromsgrove Local Life no. 38 [c 1995]

Golf 6/8/1897

Golfiana vol. 6 no. 1, 1994

Annuals and Yearbooks

The Golfer's Handbook

Golfer's Yearbook

Ladies' Golf Union Official Yearbook

Nisbet's Golf Year Book

Golfing Annual

Journals

Berrow's Worcester Journal

Birmingham Gazette

Birmingham (later Midland) Golfer

Birmingham Post

Bromsgrove Advertiser & Messenger

Bromsgrove, Droitwich and Redditch Weekly Messenger

Journals cont.

Daily Telegraph
Droitwich Guardian and Brine Baths Record
Golf
Golfiana
Golf Illustrated
Golfing Gentlewoman
Golf Monthly
London Rotarian
Sport and Play and Wheel Life
The Strand Magazine
Times Higher Educational Supplement
Worcester Evening News
Worcestershire Chronicle

Libraries, Museums and Record Offices used:

Birmingham City Council Education Department
Birmingham Reference Library
British Golf Museum, St. Andrews
British Library
British Library: Colindale Newspaper Library
Bromsgrove Library
Droitwich Library
Hereford & Worcester County Record Office
Ladies' Golf Union, St Andrews
University of Birmingham Library
University of Birmingham: Geography Department Map Library
Worcester Evening News Library
Worcester Library

References

1 *The Nature of History*, 1970, p144
2 An unattributed saying, but it is often quoted at the dinners of Sports History Societies
3 Professor David Wightman's archives
4 Droitwich Guardian 23/1/1904
5 *Strand Magazine*, London, 1906 p587
6 Droitwich Guardian 28/11/1896
7 Handbook *Droitwich as a Resort for Health and Pleasure*
8 *The Growth of Golf in Britain* 1890-1914 Golfiana, vol. 6 no. 1, 1994
9 Barbara Middlemass & Joe Hunt *John Corbett Pillar of Salt 1817-1901*, Droitwich, 1985, p90
10 Droitwich Guardian 24/11/1945: Dr. J.K. St. Joseph F.S.A. *Roman Droitwich*
11 For further reading consult *A History of Golf in Britain*, London , 1952 pp43-44 - *The Early History of British Golf*
12 Peter Ricketts *The Road to Weatheroak*, Worcestershire 1992, pp73-74. See also Garnet Scott *The History of the Worcestershire Golf Club*
13 *Victoria History of the County of Worcestershire* Vol. 2 , London, 1906 p339
14 Droitwich Guardian 27/10/1917
15 John Lowerson *Sport and the English Middle Classes 1870-1914*, Manchester, 1993 p10
16 Droitwich Guardian 27/10/1917
17 Bromsgrove Droitwich & Redditch Weekly Messenger 11/5/1895
18 Droitwich Guardian 21/3/1903
19 Droitwich Guardian 1/4/1922
20 Bromsgrove Local Life no. 38 p15
21 Barbara Middlemass & Joe Hunt vid. sup. p66
22 Droitwich Guardian 6/5/1922
23 Droitwich Guardian 2/11/1907 & 21/12/1907
24 Droitwich Guardian 21/3/1903
25 ibid
26 For further reading see the above quoted article by Peter Lewis, p14 [Ref. no. 8]
27 Bruce Haley *The Healthy Body and Victorian Culture*, The Beknap Press, 1978, p1
28 Droitwich Guardian 21/3/1903
29 Golfers Handbook 1904
30 Golfing Annual XXI 1907-08, pp252-253
31 Nisbet's Golf Year Book 1907
32 Droitwich Guardian 21/3/1903
33 ibid
34 Apart from the temporary professional appointed for one month in 1897
35 Droitwich Guardian 19/1/1907
36 ibid
37 Droitwich Guardian 18/7/1908
38 Golf 18/2/1898
39 Sport & Play & Wheel Life 28/6/1924, p5
40 ibid
41 Droitwich Guardian 21/3/1903
42 Droitwich Guardian 26/3/1904
43 Droitwich Guardian 20/9/1902
44 Droitwich Guardian 19/1/1907
45 Droitwich Guardian 13/2/1909
46 Droitwich Guardian 13/3/1909
47 Droitwich Guardian 20/2/1909
48 Droitwich Guardian 21/3/1903
49 ibid
50 Professor David Wightman's archives
51 Droitwich Guardian 21/3/1903

52 Droitwich Guardian 11/2/1911

53 Richard Holt *Stanmore Golf Club1893-1993*, London, 1993 pp35-36

54 Droitwich Guardian 16/1/1915

55 Droitwich Guardian 8/1/1916

56 Droitwich Guardian 8/5/1915

57 Droitwich Guardian 29/9/1917

58 Arthur Guise-DGC tape 038

59 Droitwich Guardian 2/6/1917

60 Arthur Guise vid. sup.

61 Droitwich Guardian 15/3/1913

62 Brenda Fowler in conversation

63 Droitwich Guardian 22/5/1920

64 Droitwich Guardian 10/2/1923

65 Droitwich Guardian 9/4/1921

66 Droitwich Guardian 4/6/1921

67 Droitwich Guardian 11/2/1922

68 Droitwich Guardian 10/2/1923

69 Droitwich Guardian 17/11/1923

70 Droitwich Guardian 15/3/1924

71 Droitwich Guardian 21/9/1956

72 Berrows Worcester Journal 6/6/1925

73 *The Game* vol. 1, London, 1980, p311

74 Birmingham Post 1/6/1925

75 DGC Tape 022-023 (*Pop* Lewis & Bernard Preston)

76 Droitwich Guardian 13/2/1937

77 Geoff Bill DGC Tape 003-004

78 Droitwich Guardian 22/6/1929

79 Birmingham Gazette 17/5/1932

80 Droitwich Guardian 13/2/1937

81 He won the title at Northfield

82 Sport & Play & Wheel Life 21/4/1923

83 Sport & Play & Wheel Life 22/8/1925

84 Droitwich Guardian 6/6/1925

85 Bromsgrove, Droitwich & Redditch Weekly Messenger 6/6/1925

86 Peter Fry *The Whitcombes*, Worcestershire, 1994 p97

87 F. Donaldson *P.G. Wodehouse - a biography*, London, 1982 p135

88 Bernard Darwin *The World that Fred Made*, London, 1955 pp221-224

89 The London Rotarian 25/8/1937

90 Michael Hobbs *British Open Champions*, London, 1991 p33

91 Arthur Guise received this information from Eric Belk, the former Editor of the Bromsgrove Messenger

92 John Freeman DGC Tape 009

93 Derek Platts DGC Tape 019

94 Droitwich Guardian 23/11/1935

95 Ron Wall was Captain in 1970 and President from 1980-1981

96 DGC Tape 003-004

97 The Corbett Trustees took up 1,000 shares amd the individual members 128

98 Droitwich Guardian 12/2/1938

99 Brackie's Notes p5

100 Cecil Everton; DGC Tape 005-006

101 In fact Ben Croydon died in 1944

102 Brackie's Notes pp5-6

103 Brackie's Notes pp6-7

104 The list is not meant to be exclusive. Geoff Bill, for example, should obviously be included

105 John was Captain from 1951-55 and President from 1971-72. Mary was Lady President from 1967-79

106 Droitwich Guardian 10/6/1939

107 DGC Tape 014

108 Bromsgrove Advertiser 11/11/1944

109 Droitwich Guardian 22/1/1960

110 Ron Wall, Greens Chairman for ten years, deserves no little credit for this improvement and for the way it was done

111 Aged only 51

112 Hamish Macdonald DGC Tape 027

113 Gen. Comm. Minutes 27/7/1977

114 Richard Holt vid. sup. p10

115 Droitwich Guardian 18/3/1939

116 In Oct. 1994

117 Geoff Bill DGC Tape 003-004

118 Member of the Worcestershire Golf Club

119 The Rev. F.D. Richardson in the Droitwich Guardian 21/3/1903

120 Daily Telegraph 2/9/1908

121 Sport & Play 10/1/1903 pp3-4

122 Droitwich Guardian 1/2/1952

123 Harold Platts was son-in-law to *skipper* Frederick Sharples (Capt. 1930, 1936 & 1937)

124 Jack Russell DGC Tape 020

125 Droit Guard 13/4/1956

126 Ladies EGM 1941

127 Mrs. G.M. Stretton-Cox

128 Balfour was Conservative Prime Minister from 1902-1905. The quote comes from *The Humours of Golf*, the Badminton Library, 1890